I LOST MY JOB
TO AI...
NOW WHAT?

NAVIGATING THE CHANGING JOB MARKET IN THE AGE OF ARTIFICIAL INTELLIGENCE

BY ANTHONY LUMPKIN

I LOST MY JOB TO AI
Navigating the AI-Driven Job Market

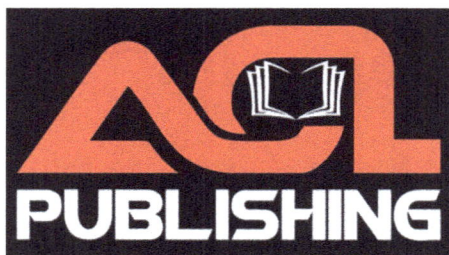

Anthony Lumpkin

Title: "I Lost My Job to AI...Now What?"
Subtitle: Navigating the AI-Driven Job Market
Author: Anthony Lumpkin
Publication Date: May 2023
Publisher: ACL Publishing
ISBN (Hardcover): 978-1-7371443-5-9
ISBN (Paperback): 978-1-7371443-6-6
Language: English
Format: Hardcover, Paperback, eBook, Audiobook
Page Count: 126
Dimensions: 7 x 10 inches
Weight: [Weight] ounces

Classification:
Library of Congress Classification: HD30.2 .L86 2023
Library of Congress Subject Headings (LCSH):
Artificial intelligence--Economic aspects
Labor market--Effect of technological innovations on
Job hunting
Career development
Occupations--Forecasting
Dewey Decimal Classification: 331.12 (Labor economics - Labor market)
BISAC (Book Industry Standards and Communications) Subject Headings:
BUS038000 BUSINESS & ECONOMICS / Careers / General
BUS030000 BUSINESS & ECONOMICS / Human Resources & Personnel
Management
COM040000 COMPUTERS / Artificial Intelligence

<u>Acknowledgments</u>

The writing of a book is a group effort, and I would want to express my gratitude to the many people who have supported me during the process of writing this book.

I would want to begin by expressing my gratitude to my family for the unending love and support they have shown me. The importance of their support and understanding to my ability to continue working on this project cannot be overstated.

I would also like to express my appreciation to the several professionals and working professionals who were kind enough to share their expertise and experience with me. The contributions of their thoughts and viewpoints have made this work significantly better.

To conclude, I would like to express my gratitude to the readers of this book for their interest in the subject matter as well as their desire to engage with the various concepts and tactics that are outlined in this publication. It is my sincere wish that you will find value in reading this book and that it will assist you in overcoming the obstacles and capitalizing on the opportunities presented by an AI-driven labor market so that you can establish a successful and satisfying career in the years to come.

Thank you.

FOREWORD

I can attest to the transformative potential of cutting-edge technology as someone who has spent the most of their career on the cutting edge of technical developments. I have, however, also seen the harm that technology can do to both our nation's economy and our daily lives.

I am glad to see that a book has been written that looks at how AI is affecting employment because of this. The authors do a great job of analyzing the various ways that AI is changing the employment market, and they offer employees helpful guidance as they negotiate this new reality.

The authors stress that the consequences of AI on employment are already taking place and are not just a theoretical idea in the far future. Since machines are more effective than humans in terms of quality, cost, and precision, workers across a wide range of businesses and professions are at risk of being replaced by them. But there is some hope in the book as well. The authors advise people to pursue more education, pick up new skills, remain adaptive, look into alternative career pathways, and support legislation that safeguard employees in order to be better prepared for the challenges offered by a job market driven by AI.

Anyone interested in the future of work, whether they are employees worried about how AI will affect their jobs, company leaders attempting to adjust to the new reality, or anyone else, should read this book. Anyone interested in the future of work should read I Lost My Job to AI...Now What? I applaud the authors for their perceptive viewpoints, thorough analyses, and unrelenting dedication to helping workers stay relevant in the modern workplace.

Debra B.

PREFACE

The development of artificial intelligence (AI) is bringing about a sea change in the working world at a rate that is unparalleled. AI has the ability to change many different industries and generate new opportunities for innovation and growth. Despite these benefits, AI also presents substantial concerns for employees whose employment are at risk of becoming automated due to the rise of AI.

I know firsthand how intimidating and hard it can be to navigate this fast shifting landscape since I have personally experienced the emotional and practical repercussions of being laid off from a job. When I was laid off due to the rise of AI, I felt hopeless and unsure of what the future held for me. Yet as time went on, I became aware of the many resources and tactics that are available to assist workers in preparing for the impact that AI will have on their occupations and adapting to these changes.

This book is an all-encompassing guide that helps workers who have lost their jobs as a result of artificial intelligence manage the difficult adjustment that they are facing. It provides practical advice and actionable strategies for coping with the emotional fallout of job loss, taking stock of one's skills and experience, exploring alternative career paths, upskilling and retraining for the future, discovering new job opportunities, and building resilience and adaptability in the face of ongoing AI disruption.

This book provides those who are struggling to find their way in the new world of work with inspiration and hope through the stories of real people who have successfully navigated the impact that AI has had on their careers. The stories are told by people who have successfully navigated the impact of AI on their careers. This book is for you if you are just beginning to experience the influence that AI will have on your job or if you have already lost your job due to automation.

I have a lot of faith that this book will prove to be an important resource for employees who are willing to take charge of their professional lives and flourish in an era that is ruled by AI. I wanted to share the knowledge and insights that I have acquired along the trip, so I created a book to help others who are I have a lot of faith that this book will help others who are I wanted to share the knowledge and insights that I have received throughout the journey.

Best, Anthony Lumpkin

Contents

Introduction

Voice assistants, self-driving cars, medical diagnosis, and financial analysis are just a few examples of the ways that the development of artificial intelligence (AI) has altered the environment in which we live. However, as AI technology progresses, it is also bringing about significant changes in the labor market. These shifts can be a source of anxiety for many individuals who worry that their jobs will be taken over by robots.

Anyone whose employment has been touched by AI, or who is concerned about the future of work, should read this book, which is titled "I Lost My Job to AI...Now What?" It is a survival guide for those individuals. Its goal is to enlighten readers on artificial intelligence (AI), its influence on the labor market, and specific actions they can take to adjust to the changes and succeed in a world in which AI is becoming increasingly commonplace.

This book's objective is to provide readers with the information and resources they require to successfully traverse the obstacles provided by artificial intelligence (AI). The emotional toll of losing a job to AI as well as guidance on how to transition to a new professional path will be discussed, along with the skills that are necessary to succeed in an economy driven by AI.

It is absolutely essential that we have a solid understanding of the changes that artificial intelligence brings with it and that we adapt accordingly as its influence continues to expand. We believe that with the help of this book, the readers will be able to tackle the difficulties of the future of work with confidence and develop a career that is both rewarding and successful in a world that is driven by AI.

In the next chapters, we will discuss how artificial intelligence (AI) is affecting the job market, the competencies and mindsets that are required to thrive in this new environment, as well as tactics for navigating the job market and finding work that is important to you. In addition to this, we will talk about the potential benefits of AI as well as the chances it provides for people to innovate and prosper in new industries.

Our goal is not to instill worry or dread in readers about the future of work; rather, it is to offer concrete counsel and direction that will assist them in preparing for and embracing the changes that are on the horizon. We are of the opinion that anyone, armed with the appropriate mentality, the appropriate tools, and the appropriate information, is capable of constructing a successful and rewarding profession in this age of AI.

Voice assistants and self-driving cars are just two examples of the numerous ways that artificial intelligence (AI) has made its way into our everyday lives. There are many other ways that AI has made its way into our lives as well. The advancements in artificial intelligence have drastically changed the manner in which we live and work, yet along with these achievements comes an entirely new set of challenges. The proliferation of artificial intelligence is causing upheavals in the employment market, which is causing worry among workers who are fearful of being replaced by robots in their roles. This concern is pushing the employment market to move, which is causing the development of artificial intelligence.

It's no secret that artificial intelligence (AI) has already started having an effect on the employment market, and this influence is only going to grow in the years to come. In point of fact, a study that was conducted by the World Economic Forum found that by the year 2025, machines will undertake more activities in the workplace than humans. This is a future that many workers find unsettling because they worry that they will fall behind in an economy that is undergoing rapid transformation.

This book, "I Lost My Job to AI...Now What?," is a how-to manual for those who have seen their employment prospects diminished as a result of AI or who are otherwise scared of the future. aims to educate its readers about AI by explaining the technology's inner workings and the impact it's having on the job market. The book's primary contribution is to provide its readers with the practical steps they need to take to survive and thrive in a world where artificial intelligence is rapidly expanding in scope and influence.

The content of the book is presented in a series of chapters that, collectively, address a wide variety of subjects connected to AI and the future of work. The first few chapters of this book walk readers through the fundamentals of artificial intelligence (AI) as well as the ways in which AI is already influencing the employment market. It also discusses the mental and emotional toll that losing a job to AI may take on individuals and offers advice on how to cope with these challenging circumstances.

The chapters in the middle of the book go into the competencies and mindsets that are essential in order to thrive in an economy that is driven by AI. These chapters investigate the technical, interpersonal, and learning qualities that will be required for professionals to succeed in a labor market driven by AI. These abilities will be crucial for professionals to have. It also brings to light the need of having a growth mentality, which means that individuals should always be willing to take on new challenges and learn from their previous experiences.

The last chapters of the book focus on the tactics and strategies that people, businesses, and society as a whole may employ in order to better prepare for a world in which AI and automation play a more dominant role. Among these are school reform, upskilling of the workforce, and planning for the workforce. The book also investigates the potential for new businesses and lines of work to crop up as a direct result of advances in AI, which would necessitate the acquisition of new competencies and information.

Because the effects of artificial intelligence (AI) are only going to become more significant as time goes on, it is absolutely necessary for us to get an awareness of the changes that AI inevitably brings about and adapt our behavior accordingly. With the assistance of this book, we hope that readers will be able to confidently face the challenges of the future of work and establish a career that is both successful and rewarding in a world that is driven by AI. We have written this book in the hopes that it will help readers achieve these goals.

Chapter 1
The Rise of AI: How We Got Here

The history of artificial intelligence (AI) is a story of innovation, desire, and the human quest for knowledge. In this chapter, we will look at where AI came from, how it has grown, and how it has changed the job market. If we know how we got to where we are now with AI, we can better plan for the future and adjust to the changes it will bring.

Pioneers and Visionaries in the Early Days of AI

AI has been thought of since ancient times when stories were told about automatons and mythical beings with intelligence like that of humans. The modern age of AI, on the other hand, started in the middle of the 20th century, when mathematician and logician Alan Turing came up with the idea of a machine that could mimic any human intelligence. In his 1950 work "Computing Machinery and Intelligence," Turing came up with the Turing Test, which is still used as a standard for artificial intelligence (AI) today.

In the 1950s and 1960s, there was a lot of interest in AI study. This was partly because electronic computers were becoming more common. Early artificial intelligence programs like Samuel's checkers player and Newell and Simon's Logic Theorist showed that machines could do things that used to require human ability. AI experts were hopeful and thought that within a few decades, a fully sentient AI would be built.

But AI study stopped moving forward in the 1970s and 1980s because there wasn't enough money and computers couldn't do much at the time. During this time, which is called the "AI Winter," study into AI slowed down and attention turned to other areas of computer science.

The Rise of AI: How Data and Algorithms Can Help

In the 1990s, when the internet became popular, there was a huge increase in the amount of data that was available. This data became a key resource for the growth of AI. With this huge pool of data and improvements in computer hardware and processing power, researchers were able to make more complex algorithms and teach AI models to be more accurate.

In the late 1990s and early 2000s, AI study got a boost from the development of machine learning, which is a branch of AI that focuses on giving machines

the ability to learn and change on their own. Deep learning is a type of machine learning that uses artificial neural networks to mimic the way the human brain processes information. People like Geoffrey Hinton, Yann LeCun, and Yoshua Bengio were early leaders in this field.

Deep learning has been shown to be very good at handling hard problems, like recognizing images and speech, processing natural language, and playing games. In 2012, Hinton's team at the University of Toronto won the ImageNet Large Scale Visual Recognition Challenge. This showed how powerful deep learning can be for computer vision tasks. After this breakthrough, people became interested in AI study again and put money into it.

As AI kept getting better, it hit new milestones that showed how much it could do. In 1997, IBM's Deep Blue beat Garry Kasparov, who was the world champion at chess. This showed that AI could learn complex strategy games. In 2011, IBM's Watson won the game show Jeopardy! This showed how far AI has come in understanding natural words and finding information.

AI made a lot of progress in the 2010s, thanks to the coming together of big data, powerful tools, and new algorithms. In 2015, Lee Sedol, the world champion Go player, lost to Google DeepMind's AlphaGo. This made news around the world. Unlike chess, the game Go has a huge number of possible moves, which makes it hard for AI to play. The victory of AlphaGo changed how people thought about AI's possibilities.

AI has also made a lot of progress in the area of self-driving cars. Companies like Tesla, Waymo, and Cruise are making more and more advanced technology for self-driving cars. In 2015, Tesla released its Autopilot feature, which gave drivers advanced driver-aid systems like adaptive cruise control and the ability to stay in their lane. Waymo started its Waymo One self-driving taxi service in Arizona in 2018. This was the start of a new era in transportation.

AI in the Workplace: From Help to Trouble

As AI got better, it started to be used in more and more ways in the workplace. At first, AI was seen as a way to boost output and do things like data entry and analysis automatically. But as AI became more advanced, it started to take over jobs that needed more skill and knowledge.

For example, AI algorithms have made big strides in the field of finance, where they are used for everything from catching scams and figuring out credit scores to algorithmic trading and managing portfolios. In healthcare, AI-powered diagnosis tools and image analysis have shown that they may be better than human experts. This has made people worry about the future of jobs in these fields.

At the same time, AI has also given human workers new ways to do their jobs. For example, AI-driven data analysis has led to the creation of the job of a "data scientist," whose job is to use their knowledge to get insights from big datasets and make predictions based on them. In the same way, the increasing use of AI in the workplace has led to a need for AI ethics specialists, who help make sure that AI apps are built and used in a responsible way.

What AI Means for the Job Market

The rise of AI has led to a discussion about how it will affect the job market. Some experts say that AI will put a lot of people out of work as computers take over jobs that humans used to do. Others say that AI will create new jobs and businesses, which will lead to a net increase in jobs.

No matter what happens in the end, it is clear that AI is changing the job market in big ways. The "Future of Jobs Report 2020" from the World Economic Forum says that AI and technology will take 85 million jobs away by 2025, while 97 million new jobs will be made.

This change in the job market will have big effects on workers, who will need to learn how to use new tools and get new skills to stay useful in an AI-driven economy. As the AI revolution moves forward, it is important for people and lawmakers to understand the changes it will bring and make plans for how to handle the change.

AI has come a long way thanks to human creativity, technological growth, and a never-ending need to understand the world around us. As AI keeps getting better, it will bring workers and society as a whole both challenges and possibilities.

In the parts that follow, we'll talk about the emotional effects of losing a job to AI, how to adapt to the new job market driven by AI, and how to thrive in a world that is becoming more and more automated. By learning about AI's past and future, we can be better prepared for the changes it will bring and help shape a future that is fair, inclusive, and full of opportunities for everyone.

Chapter 2

The Emotional Impact: Dealing with Job Loss

I t's hard and upsetting to lose a job, especially when it's because of things we can't control, like the rise of AI and robotics. In this chapter, we'll talk about the emotional effects of losing a job, give you ways to deal with it, and answer some of the most common questions about the emotional journey to a better future. By recognizing and working through the feelings that come with losing a job, we can put ourselves in a better position to change, grow, and do well in the changing job market.

How the emotional roller coaster works

It's normal to feel a range of feelings when you lose your job, from shock and disbelief to anger, fear, and sadness. When the cause of job loss is something as vague and hard to stop as AI, these feelings can be amplified. It's important to realize that these feelings are real and that working through them is a necessary step toward moving on.

Shock and denial: When someone loses their job, they often feel shocked and like they can't fully understand what's going on. Denial can be a short-term way to deal with a problem, giving us time to adjust to the truth of our situation.

Anger and Frustration: When the truth of losing a job hits, you may feel angry and frustrated. It's normal to feel angry at the things that caused people to lose their jobs or at the people who made the AI-driven changes happen.

Fear and Anxiety: If you lose your job, you might feel afraid and worried about the future. You might worry about finding a new job, keeping your finances stable, and adjusting to a new work path.

Sadness and grief:

Losing a job can make us feel sad and upset because we miss our professional identity, our daily schedule, and the social connections we had through our old job.

Acceptance and Hope:

As we work through the emotional effects of losing a job, we can finally reach a point of acceptance and hope, where we accept the reality of our situation and start to see opportunities for growth and positive change.

Ways to deal with the loss of a job:

Even though there is no one way to deal with the mental effects of losing a job, the following tips can help make the process easier to handle and build resilience during hard times;

Recognize and accept your feelings:

Give yourself the freedom to feel and talk about how you feel. Recognizing and validating your feelings is a key step in dealing with the mental effects of losing your job.

Seek Support:

Reach out for mental support and advice from friends, family, and trained counselors. Joining support groups or networking communities for people in similar situations can also help you feel less alone and give you useful information from people who have also lost their jobs.

Maintain a Routine:

In times of change, having a daily routine can help provide structure and a feeling of normalcy. Include things that are good for your health, like working out, eating well, and getting enough sleep.

Pay attention to what you can change:

Even though it may be tempting to think about what happened to make you lose your job, focusing on what you can change, like updating your resume, learning new skills, and networking, can help you feel less powerless and anxious.

Learn to be kind to yourself: Be kind and patient with yourself as you go through this hard time. Realize that losing a job is common and that you can get back on your feet and find new possibilities.

Set Goals That Can Be Met:

Make your job search and work change into smaller goals that you can reach. This will help you stay on track, keep you inspired, and make you feel like you're making progress.

Questions People Usually Ask

How long until I feel better after I've lost my job?

How a person heals emotionally after losing a job depends on the person. The length and intensity of feelings can be affected by things like a person's strength, their network of support, and their own life circumstances. It's important to be patient with yourself and realize that it's normal for the process to take time. You will start to feel better and more hopeful about the future as you work through your feelings and take steps toward a new job path.

I Lost My job because of AI. Is it normal to feel bad about it?

Yes, people who have lost their jobs because of AI and technology often feel guilty. But it's important to remember that losing your job is caused by larger economic and technological trends and not by your own worth or skills. Instead of thinking about how bad you are, try to put your energy into finding new chances and building a better future.

How can I stay upbeat while I'm looking for a job?

During a job search, it can be hard to stay upbeat, especially if you are feeling sad about losing your job. Think about the following ways to keep a happy attitude:

Focus on the good things in your life and tell others how thankful you are for what you have.

Stay in touch with people: keep in touch with friends and family who are there for you and can offer help and support.

Deal with stress: You can reduce stress by doing things like meditation, deep breathing exercises, and regular physical movement.

Honor even small victories: Recognize and enjoy the small steps you take toward getting a job, like getting an interview or learning a new skill.

What if I'm having a hard time dealing with the mental effects of losing my job?

If you can't handle the mental effects of losing your job on your own, you might want to talk to a therapist or counselor for help. These experts can give you helpful advice and support, helping you deal with the emotional challenges that come with losing your job and finding ways to deal with stress and anxiety.

It can be hard and challenging to deal with the emotional effects of losing a job, especially when the job market is changing quickly because of AI and technology. By recognizing and working through the feelings that come with losing a job, getting help, and putting your attention on growth and resilience, you can get through this tough time and come out stronger and better prepared for the future.

In the next few chapters, we'll talk about ways to adapt to the new AI-driven job market, figure out your skills, and build a satisfying career in the age of AI. If you understand and deal with the mental effects of losing your job, you will be better able to accept change and take advantage of the chances that lie ahead.

Chapter 3

Embracing Change: Adopting a Growth Mindset

In a world where AI and automation are causing people to lose their jobs, it's important to have a growth mindset in order to succeed in the new job market and take advantage of chances for personal and professional growth. In this chapter, we'll talk about the idea of a growth mindset, its benefits, and some easy ways to develop one. We will also talk about the pros and cons of different ways to adapt to change in an AI-driven job market.

How to Get a Growth Mindset

Carol Dweck, a psychologist, came up with the idea of a "growth mindset." She said that our views about our intelligence and abilities have a big effect on our motivation, effort, and, in the end, success. A growth mindset is a belief that intelligence, talents, and skills can be developed and improved through commitment, hard work, and persistence.

A fixed mindset, on the other hand, says that intelligence and skills are static and can't change much. People with a fixed mindset may avoid challenges, give up quickly when they face problems, and feel threatened by the success of others.

Advantages of Having a Growth Mindset

Having a growth attitude can be helpful in many ways, especially when facing the challenges and unknowns of a job market driven by AI. Among these advantages are:

Increased Motivation: A growth mindset pushes people to focus on learning and getting better, which can make them more motivated and engaged when they face problems.

Resilience: Believing that skills can be learned helps people get over failures and keep a positive attitude when things are hard.

Adaptability: A growth mindset encourages people to be open to change and adjust to new situations, which is important in a job market that is always changing.

Research has shown that people with a growth mindset tend to do better than those with a fixed mindset because they are more likely to keep going when things get hard and look for ways to grow.

Strategies and approaches for developing a growth mindset

The following tips can help you develop a growth mindset and put yourself in a better situation to succeed in an AI-driven job market:

Accept Challenges: Look for ways to grow and learn, even if they take you out of your comfort zone. Taking on challenges can help you build resilience and faith in your ability to adapt and grow.

Learn from Failure: Instead of seeing mistakes and failures as signs of how limited you are, see them as lessons you can learn from. Think about what you can learn from these things and how you can use this information in the future.

Seek Feedback: Ask others for feedback and see it as a chance to improve, not as a criticism of your skills. Feedback that is helpful can help you find places to improve and learn new skills.

Look at the steps: Focus on how you are learning and getting better, not just on the end result. This change in mindset can help you enjoy and be happy with what you're doing more, as well as be more persistent and strong.

Surround yourself with people who have a growth mindset. Talk to people who share your growth mindset and can help you deal with the difficulties of the AI-driven job market.

Approaches to Embracing Change: Pros and Cons

In this part, we'll look at different ways to accept change in an AI-driven job market and talk about the pros and cons of each.

Approach 1: Adding skills and learning all the time

Upskilling and continuous learning are ways to stay relevant and competitive in the job market by gaining new skills and information.

Pros:

- It makes people more employable and flexible.
- Making jobs safer gives people new job chances
- Encourages growth and progress of the individual

Cons:

- Can take a lot of time and be hard to juggle with other tasks

- May need a lot of money spent on classes or training programs

- There's no promise that new skills will lead to jobs right away.

Approach 2: Changing jobs

A career change is when you move to a new field or business, usually because you want new challenges, more personal satisfaction, or better job opportunities.

Pros:

- Chance to try out new hobbies and talents

- Possibility for more personal and job happiness

- Access to new business networks and connections

- May lead to more job security in a job market that is changing quickly.

Cons:

- Can be dangerous and could cause financial instability at first

- It takes time and work to learn new skills and information.

- May mean starting in a new area at a lower position or salary

- Possible age discrimination or trouble getting into a new field

Approach 3: Being an entrepreneur.

Entrepreneurship means starting and running your own business. This gives you a chance to be creative and follow your own interests.

Pros:

- Control and independence over your work and job

- Chance to be creative and come up with new ideas

- You can make as much as you want.

- Possibility of giving other people jobs

Cons:

- Risk to money and the chance of failing

- needs a lot of time and money to be spent on it.

- High amounts of responsibility and stress

- There is no promise of success or security

Approach 4: Freelancing and the Gig Economy

Freelancing and being a part of the gig economy involve working as an independent contractor or self-employed person and offering services to multiple clients or organizations.

Pros:

- Freedom to choose where and when to work

- chance to get money from different places

- Depending on skills and experience, there is a chance to make more money.

- enables people to specialize in a certain skill or area

Cons:

- Not having job security or perks

- Unstable income and the possibility of financial instability

- Requires self-discipline and good time management

- There may be times when there's a lot of competition for jobs.

Adopting a growth attitude is important if you want to deal with the challenges and unknowns of a job market driven by AI. People can not only survive technological disruption but also succeed in it if they are open to change, keep learning, and are flexible.

In the next few chapters, we'll talk about real-world ways to find and use your unique strengths, build a satisfying job in the age of AI, and make sure you're ready to take advantage of the opportunities that lie ahead.

By knowing the pros and cons of different ways to embrace change, you can make smart choices about the best way forward for your job and personal growth, which will lead to a more satisfying and successful future.

Chapter 4
Identifying Your Strengths and Opportunities: A Data-Driven Approach

With artificial intelligence and automation reshaping the work market, it's more important than ever to zero in on your own set of skills, passions, and development areas. In the context of an AI-driven labor market, this chapter will examine a data-driven method for evaluating your abilities and pinpointing areas for improvement. We will assist you through the process of building a spreadsheet to organize your findings, helping you make educated decisions regarding your professional path.

Step 1: Take Stock of Your Talents and Hobbies

Evaluate your current level of expertise, interests, and experience. Think about your hard skills, like technical know-how or industry expertise, and your soft skills, like the ability to communicate, lead, and solve problems. Consider your hobbies and interests too, as these may point you in the direction of a rewarding profession.

Make a spreadsheet and include in the first column all of your identified talents, hobbies, and experiences. Using a scale from 1 to 5, with 5 being the highest level of expertise or interest, please rate each item in the second column.

Example Spreadsheet:

Skill/Interest	Rating
Graphic Design	4
Coding	3
Sales	2
Writing	5
Photography	1

Step 2: Research Job Market Trends

The following step is to examine projected growth sectors and occupations in the existing job market. Job boards, industry studies, and labor market statistics are all good places to start looking for relevant information. Write down the tendencies that you find most interesting and relevant to your expertise and hobbies.

Create a new sheet in your spreadsheet to document the employment patterns you've observed. In the second column, rank the trends from most relevant to least relevant to your expertise and interests.

Example Spreadsheet:

Job Market Trend	Rating
Remote Work Opportunities	4
Digital Marketing	3
Renewable Energy	2
Data Analysis	1
Content Creation	5

Step 3: Identify Skills Gaps and Opportunities for Growth

Evaluate how well your unique set of abilities and interests align with the emerging trends in the work market. Investigate potential growth and development possibilities by identifying skill gaps and places where your abilities coincide with in-demand sectors or roles.

Create a new column for your interests and skills in your spreadsheet. Check the box next to each skill or interest if it relates to a current hiring trend. (Yes or No). Find any areas of weakness in your skill set that may need to be improved.

Example Spreadsheet:

Skill/Interest	Rating	Market Trend Alignment	Skills Gap
Graphic Design	4	Yes	No
Coding	3	No	Yes
Sales	2	Yes	Yes
Writing	5	Yes	No
Photography	1	No	No

Step 4: Develop an Action Plan

Create a strategy to improve your weaknesses, fill up your skill gaps, and take advantage of employment market openings based on your research. Objectives for this strategy could include things like taking specialized classes, expanding a resume, or making connections in a certain field.

Create a new sheet in your spreadsheet to record your plans of action. For added accountability, set a due date next to each task in the second column.

Example Spreadsheet:

Goal/Action Item	Target Completion Date
Complete a digital marketing course	2023-07-01
Build a professional writing portfolio	2023-09-01
Attend a renewable energy conference	2023-10-15
Network with professionals in sales	Ongoing
Learn advanced coding techniques	2024-01-01

Step 5: Monitor Progress and Reassess

Maintain a spreadsheet to track your progress as you check off completed tasks and achieve milestones. Keep your talents, interests, and knowledge current with the trends in the employment market by regularly reviewing your action plan.

Consider updating your resume every so often to reflect your evolving set of abilities, hobbies, and the state of the employment market. You can stay ahead of the curve and adapt to the AI-driven employment market by regularly updating and improving your action plan.

Finding your own unique skills and development prospects is more important than ever in this age of artificial intelligence and automation. Using a data-driven approach and the analytical power of spreadsheets, you can choose the best course of action for your career and ensure your continued success in a dynamic labor market.

In the following chapters, we'll discuss how to construct a successful profession in the age of AI through techniques including networking, personal branding, and utilizing digital platforms to advertise your abilities. In the AI-driven job market, knowing your skills and where you can improve will put you in the best position to succeed and seize the amazing chances that await you.

Chapter 5

Exploring New Opportunities: AI-Resistant Careers

Although the advent of AI and automation has caused widespread upheaval in the labor market, it has also paved the way for novel occupations that are less amenable to robotic replacement. In this upbeat and encouraging section, we'll talk about occupations that are resilient to artificial intelligence, industries that are thriving in spite of technological progress, and how to break into and thrive in these expanding fields.

Learning Professions That Can Withstand Artificial Intelligence

Professions that are "AI-resistant" are ones that will not be negatively impacted by automation in the near future. Creativity, empathy, complicated problem-solving, and the ability to relate with others are just a few of the human qualities necessary for many of these positions. You may secure a steady and rewarding job in the middle of the continuing technological transformation by specializing in one of these AI-resistant fields.

Despite the development of AI and automation, many sectors are expanding and need for skilled workers. The following are examples of such sectors:

Healthcare: With an aging population and rising need for medical treatment, the healthcare industry is in need of qualified individuals to fill a wide range of positions, including nurses, doctors, therapists, and administrators. Empathy, emotional intelligence, and interpersonal skills are typically required for these positions, which are difficult for computers to simulate.

Artistic Disciplines: Artificial intelligence has replaced humans in some creative roles, but it has a long way to go before it can fully replace human imagination. Graphic design, advertising, writing, and the arts are all fields that continue to place a premium on individual creativity and originality.

Education: The role of educators, trainers, and coaches in shaping future generations is vital. These positions call for an in-depth knowledge of human emotions, empathy, and the capacity to adapt instructional methods to each student's unique learning style, all of which are difficult for AI to imitate.

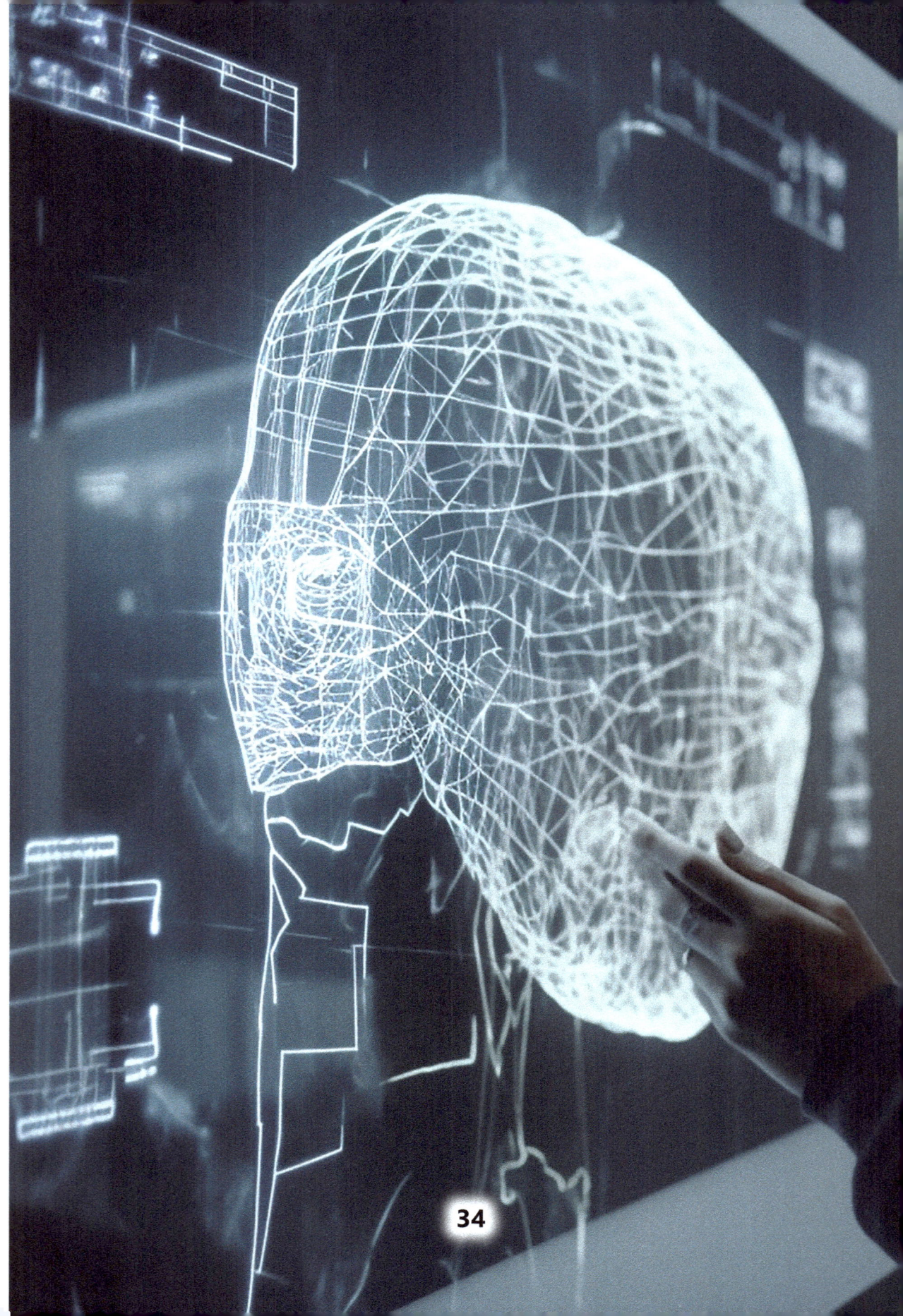

Construction, plumbing, and electrical work are examples of skilled crafts that have shown to be resistant to automation. Jobs in this field typically necessitate in-depth training, practical experience, and flexibility.

Positions in counseling, social work, and community outreach all call on people skills such as empathy, compassion, and the capacity to connect with others on a deep and genuine level. There is little chance that artificial intelligence will ever be able to replace these abilities.

Choosing a Profession that Won't Get Replaced by Robots

Follow these steps to find work that won't be taken over by robots:

Take Stock of Your Talents and Hobbies: Think about the things that make you, you. What do you do for fun and satisfaction? How do these jobs and fields interact with those that are safe from automation?

Do your homework and network extensively Discover more about the fields and professions that pique your interest. You can gain useful information and learn about new prospects by networking with experts in these fields.

Investigate Educational and Training Options: Look into schools and programs that offer the training you need to enter your chosen AI-resistant profession.

Acquire Real-World Experience: Look for internships, part-time jobs, or volunteer opportunities in your field of study.

Putting Your Skills on Display Through Online Mediums

Finding jobs that can't be done by AI is only half the battle; you also need to find ways to show off your abilities in the digital realm. Here are some methods to help you establish a solid online identity:

Create a personal website to feature your work, resume, and other relevant information. Make sure your site is user-friendly, has a good design, and conveys your identity.

Make use of social media sites such as LinkedIn, Twitter, and Facebook to make contacts in your sector, disseminate your work, and monitor developments in your industry.

Connect with Virtual Groups and Forums:

Take Part in Online Communities

You may build your reputation as an informed and involved professional while also meeting new people and gaining insight from those more experienced than you.

Developing and disseminating information (like blog posts, articles, or videos) that demonstrates your mastery of your field is an important part of point (d). This might boost your credibility as an expert and interest of prospective employers or customers.

Participate in webinars and virtual events pertaining to your field to learn about emerging trends, network with other experts, and broaden your perspective.

Taking on a "Growth Mindset"

Adopting a growth mentality that places a premium on learning and improving oneself is essential in today's AI-driven labor environment. You can have a successful and satisfying profession despite technological upheaval if you are open to change and actively seek out ways to advance your skills.

Remain Informed: Follow the most recent news and trends in artificial intelligence and automation in your field. This will allow you to better prepare for future changes and adjust your methods accordingly.

Spend time and money on furthering your education, taking classes online, or teaching yourself new things in order to fulfill b., below.

Seek input: Seek input on a regular basis from mentors, peers, and coworkers in order to pinpoint areas for development.

Remain flexible and ready to make course corrections in your professional life as circumstances demand. The capacity to change with the times and seize new possibilities is crucial in today's competitive employment environment.

In this inspiring and interesting chapter, we looked at occupations unlikely to be replaced by AI, industries expected to expand, and methods for locating and capitalizing on such opportunities. You may have a secure and rewarding career in the age of AI if you choose to specialize in areas that are less amenable to automation and use digital platforms to demonstrate your abilities.

In the following chapters, we'll get into the nitty-gritty of how to construct a successful career in today's AI-driven job market, including such essentials as networking, personal branding, and making the most of digital platforms to locate and secure employment prospects.

You may not only survive but prosper in the fast changing job landscape by being proactive, adopting a growth mindset, and focusing on AI-resistant occupations.

Chapter 6
Reinventing Yourself: A Guide to Personal Branding

Having a solid personal brand is crucial in today's competitive employment market, especially with the rise of artificial intelligence. An effective personal brand may help you get noticed, highlight your best qualities, and attract opportunities that are a good fit for you. To help you reinvent yourself and succeed in today's AI-driven job market, we'll go over the measures you can take to establish your personal brand in this chapter.

Learning About Your Own Brand

The goal of personal branding is to distinguish yourself from other professionals in your field by drawing attention to the specific set of qualities that make you stand out. With a solid reputation behind you, you can:

- Make a name for yourself as a go-to specialist.
- Capture the interest of prospective customers or business partners.
- Create a sense of reliability and authority among your intended audience.
- Boost your professional standing and connections.

Figuring Out What Makes You Special

Your personal brand is built on your UVP or unique value proposition. It emphasizes your unique set of experiences, abilities, and qualifications that set you apart from the competition.

Answer these questions to determine your unique selling proposition:

1. In what ways do you distinguish yourself from others?
2. Just what is it about you that makes you special?
3. In what ways do you stand out from the crowd?
4. For your ideal client, what difficulties can you alleviate?

Take some time to reflect on these questions and jot down your answers in the blank columns below:

Skills and Expertise	Unique Experiences	Personal Qualities	Problems You Can Solve

Creating a Trustworthy Reputation for Yourself

Consistency in your message and honesty in your presentation are two of the most important factors in developing a solid personal brand. That means:

Create a captivating statement that captures your unique value proposition (UVP) and conveys who you are in the business world. You should use this message uniformly in all of your digital profiles and promotional materials.

Be consistent in the message you send throughout all of your online properties, including your social media platforms, personal website, and other online assets. If your current profile photo, bio, and description don't reflect your brand's values, it's time to make some changes.

Sharing information that showcases your knowledge and skill in your subject is an excellent way to build your online reputation and attract potential clients. This will assist solidify your reputation as an industry expert and add value to your personal brand.

Embracing Authenticity: Show your strengths and weaknesses honestly when presenting yourself. This can make your personal brand more memorable and approachable, which in turn increases trust and engagement.

Building relationships and expanding one's professional network

Meaningful interactions serve as the cornerstone upon which a powerful personal brand is constructed. Expanding your professional network and making connections with individuals in your field can help you learn from others, discover new opportunities, and increase your professional network.

The following are some tactics that will help you network more effectively:

Take Part in Industry Events: Attending industry events, such as conferences, seminars, and other events relating to your sector, is a great way to network with other professionals in your industry and keep up with the most recent trends and innovations.

Participate in Online Communities: Participate in online forums, social media groups, or professional associations that are relevant to your industry in order to network with colleagues, exchange ideas, and obtain new perspectives.

Cultivate Meaningful Connections: Instead of focusing solely on amassing contacts, give your attention to cultivating real, long-lasting relationships with people who are already part of your network. Be willing to learn from the experiences of others while also offering assistance, support, and encouragement to others around you.

Make Use Of Social Media: Make use of social media platforms such as LinkedIn, Twitter, and Facebook in order to interact with professionals in your sector, join relevant groups, and engage in discussions. This can assist you in maintaining your awareness of current events, enhancing your online presence, and establishing meaningful connections.

Keeping an Eye on, and Making Changes to, Your Personal Brand

As you advance in your profession, your personal brand will need to change to represent your maturation and the new directions in which you want to head. It is possible to maintain the usefulness and relevance of your personal brand by evaluating and modifying it on a regular basis. The following are some suggestions for keeping an eye on and improving your personal brand:

Establish specific Objectives for Your Personal Brand: One of the first things you should do when developing your personal brand is to establish specific goals for it. These goals should include boosting your internet visibility, growing a professional network, or attracting new job chances. You'll be able to track your progress and evaluate how successful your efforts are at building your personal brand with the help of these goals.

Solicit input:

When it comes to your personal brand, you should solicit input from your peers, mentors, or professional contacts. This can assist you in recognizing areas in which you could improve and provide you with valuable insight into how people view you.

Maintain an Up-to-Date Online Presence:

Ensure that your social media profiles, personal website, and other online assets are kept up-to-date on a consistent basis to ensure that they appropriately reflect your current set of skills, experiences, and ambitions.

Stay Current:

Make sure you are up to date on the latest advancements, industry trends, and recommendations for personal branding best practices. Maintaining a cutting-edge personal brand is essential to standing out in today's fiercely competitive employment market. This can help you do just that.

Developing a powerful personal brand is one of the most important steps you can take toward reinventing yourself and flourishing in an employment market driven by AI. You may differentiate yourself from the competition and attract the opportunities you want by learning the significance of personal branding, elaborating on your one-of-a-kind value proposition, establishing a consistent and genuine online presence, and engaging in active networking and connection development. It is important to keep in mind that as you advance in your career, you should continuously analyze and modify your personal brand in order to ensure that it continues to be beneficial in assisting you in achieving your professional goals.

Chapter 7
Networking in the Age of AI: Building Meaningful Connections

Networking has taken on an increased level of significance in this age of information technology. Building meaningful connections with others can provide a competitive edge in the job market and enable professional advancement. This is especially important given the rise of artificial intelligence and other advanced technologies. This chapter will discuss the relevance of networking in the modern era, highlight best practices for creating and keeping connections, and analyze techniques for utilizing artificial intelligence and associated tools to boost your networking efforts.

The Importance of Networking in the Digital Age

Individuals are able to develop new possibilities, get insights into their sector, and foster relationships with people that are mutually advantageous when they engage in networking activities. This makes networking an essential component of professional success. In this day and age of artificial intelligence, there are several reasons why networking has taken on an even greater level of significance.

Connections are Essential: In today's world, having positive relationships with other people can provide you a competitive advantage in the job market and other areas of life.

Technology Makes Networking Easier: AI-powered platforms and other digital tools make it simpler than ever before to connect with other people, even across enormous distances.

There is an Increase in Specialization: As there is an increase in the prevalence of specialization and niche expertise, it is becoming increasingly vital to network with individuals in your profession.

Innovation Requires Collaboration: In today's quickly changing corporate scene, the capacity to cooperate and work well with others is important for innovation.

Developing Meaningful Connections Through Exemplary Methods

Building professional relationships is much more than just developing superficial connections with other people. You need to approach networking with intention and attention if you want to develop relationships that are both long-lasting and meaningful. The following are some of the most effective methods for establishing and sustaining connections:

Maintain Your Authenticity: In the long run, relationships that are built on authenticity have a greater chance of being successful. Stay true to who you are, and prioritize developing connections with others who appreciate the same things you do in life.

Put Quality, Not Quantity, First: It is not always useful to build a huge network of connections if you do not have genuine relationships with the people in that network. Instead, you should put more emphasis on the quality of the connections you build. Put your energy towards building a more intimate network with more significant relationships.

Take Care of Your Network: If you want your relationships to persist, it's critical to maintain your network and keep in regular contact with the people in it. After meeting someone for the first time, it is important to follow up with them and to make an effort to be in regular contact.

Give Back: It's important to remember that networking is a two-way street. Be kind to those in your network by sharing your time, skills, and resources, and look for opportunities to assist those who are already connected to you.

Utilizing Artificial Intelligence (AI) to Improve Networking Efforts

Platforms and solutions that are powered by AI have the potential to simplify and improve many aspects of the networking process. The following are some ways you may use to make your networking efforts more effective by utilizing AI.

Make Use of AI-Powered Platforms:

Tools such as LinkedIn and other employment platforms use AI to recommend potential connections based on a user's profile as well as the user's interests.

Use AI to Conduct Data Analysis and Identify possibilities:

AI can assist you in doing data analyses and locating prospective networking possibilities that are tailored to your interests and goals.

Automate Your Networking Efforts Using Chatbots and Other Tools:

Chatbots can assist you in managing your networking efforts by sending messages, organizing meetings, and following up with connections.

Participate in Online Communities:

Participating in online communities that are linked to your sector can help you connect with other professionals who have similar interests, and it can also keep you current on the most recent trends and advances.

In this day and age, building your professional network is critical to your professional success. You may improve the effectiveness of your networking activities and create long-lasting relationships that can benefit you in a variety of ways by cultivating meaningful connections, remaining authentic, concentrating on quality, and making use of technologies and platforms powered by artificial intelligence (AI). You may stay ahead of the curve in today's fast changing job market if you stay current on best practices for networking and include AI into your strategy.

Chapter 8

Upskilling for Success: Strategies for Continuous Learning,

In today's world, if you want to have a successful job, you need to actively participate in a wide variety of networking activities. Because of the advancements in artificial intelligence (AI), networking is today more important than it has ever been. In this chapter, we will study the effects that AI has had on networking, and we will also address how you can create meaningful connections that will assist you in achieving success in an era that is ruled by AI. Both of these topics will be covered in this chapter.

The Impact that AI Will Have on the Field of Networking

The Critical Role of Human Interaction in an Era Dominated by Artificial Intelligence Networking has always been an essential part of getting ahead in one's career, but with the rise of AI, it is now more critical than it has ever been. As a result of the proliferation of AI, both the labor market and the method in which we perform our work are undergoing substantial modifications. Cultivating strong professional relationships will assist you in keeping up with these trends and in locating new opportunities.

What Influence Does Artificial Intelligence Have on Networking?

AI is making it easier to connect with individuals from all over the world through the use of social media platforms, virtual reality, and other online networking activities. As a result of improvements in artificial intelligence (AI), chatbots and voice assistants are becoming increasingly common in the workplace. This is causing a shift in the way we communicate, as well.

Developing Realistic and Meaningful Relationships in an Era of Artificial Intelligence Developing a Strong Presence Online

For the establishment of a network in this day and age, it is of the utmost importance to have a substantial internet presence. Create a professional profile on LinkedIn and ensure that it is up to date with your most current work experience, talents, and achievements by updating it frequently after you have created the profile. Share blog posts and articles that are relevant to your sector, and start a dialogue with other professionals in your field by commenting on and sharing the knowledge they provide.

Attending and Participating in Online Events for the Purpose of Networking

The growth of artificial intelligence has resulted in an increase in the number of virtual networking events, which have also become much simpler to engage in. You should look for online events that are associated with your industry and make it a goal to participate in as many of these events as you are able to in order to create connections, as well as to get knowledge about developing trends and opportunities. Be sure that you enter each event with a clear aim in mind, whether it be to meet a specific person or to gain knowledge about a specific subject. This will ensure that you get the most out of each experience.

Developing Relationships and Expanding Professional Networks Through the Use of Social Media Platforms for social media such as Twitter and Instagram can be incredibly valuable instruments for developing relationships and expanding professional networks. Follow the influential people and thought leaders in your industry, and engage in the discussion surrounding their postings by commenting on them and sharing them with others. Utilize hashtags that are specific to your field if you want to increase the likelihood of connecting with people who share your passions and interests.

Making Use Of Tools For Networking Assisted by the use of Artificial Intelligence

By utilizing any one of a variety of distinct networking platforms that are driven by artificial intelligence, you will have the ability to communicate with various other specialists that work in your area of expertise. Utilize technology such as Crystal Knows, which employs artificial intelligence to assess personality traits and communication styles, to assist you in acquiring a deeper grasp of the most effective methods to approach and interact with a variety of people.

These technologies can help you achieve your goal of gaining a deeper understanding of the most effective ways to approach and interact with a wide range of individuals. A further illustration of this would be the app Humin, which makes use of artificial intelligence to keep track of the individuals you are affiliated with and to remind you of pertinent facts about each one of them.

Frequently Asked Questions

Is it possible for artificial intelligence to take the role of traditional networking?

No, artificial intelligence will never be able to replace good old-fashioned networking. The human element that is inherent in face-to-face contacts cannot be replicated by artificial intelligence; nonetheless, AI can be used to assist you in connecting with people and creating bonds.

What are some ways that I can make use of AI to improve my capacity to network with other people?

Utilize programs that are run by artificial intelligence, such as Crystal Knows and Humin, to enhance your capacity to comprehend a wide range of people and to connect effectively with them.

To make genuine relationships in this day and age, it is necessary to maintain an active online presence and take part in a variety of online activities and gatherings. Through the use of social media platforms like as LinkedIn, Twitter, and Instagram, you may extend your network by connecting with industry thought leaders, sharing relevant articles and blog posts, and participating in relevant conversations.

You can obtain deeper insights into communication patterns and personality features, as well as maintain track of your professional contacts, by leveraging networking tools driven by AI, such as Crystal Knows and Humin. These tools can be used in addition to social media platforms.

Frequently Asked Questions

- Is it feasible for AI to take the place of conventional forms of networking?

No, AI will not completely replace face-to-face networking any time soon. Although artificial intelligence can facilitate the building of relationships and connections with other individuals, it is not a suitable substitute for the human aspect inherent in face-to-face encounters.

- How can I increase my networking skills by using AI?

Applications that are powered by artificial intelligence such as Crystal Knows and Humin can help you better understand and communicate with other people, as well as keep track of the different professional relationships you have.

- In this age of artificial intelligence, what are some effective ways to network?

The establishment of a substantial online presence, participation in online networking events, the cultivation of connections through social media, and the utilization of networking technologies driven by AI are all helpful techniques for establishing and maintaining connections in this age of AI.

- What steps can I take to ensure that I am up to date on the newest networking advances and opportunities?

Attend virtual networking events, read journals geared specifically for your sector, and make advantage of social media to interact with thought leaders and significant persons in your area of expertise.

Examples of Effective Networking in the Age of AI John is a marketing professional who is interested in expanding his network in the age of artificial intelligence (AI). In order to network with other professionals in the business, he develops a credible profile on LinkedIn and distributes marketing-related publications and blog entries online.

- Maria is a seasoned marketing professional who has an interest in the ways in which AI might be applied to her field. She networked with top executives in the field at a conference that focused on AI and marketing, and she continues to keep in touch with them using LinkedIn and other digital tools. Eventually, she works on a research project with one of them as a collaborator.

In conclusion, constructing and sustaining meaningful connections is a vital component of professional development in this day and age of digital technology. Although artificial intelligence has fundamentally changed the way we network, it is not yet capable of completely displacing in-person encounters. However, professionals are able to expand their networks and keep up with the newest developments and trends in their sector by leveraging social media platforms, online networking events, and networking tools that are powered by artificial intelligence (AI).

Keep in mind that the quality of the connections you have is far more important than the quantity, and that developing true relationships requires both time and work. Professionals have a better chance of succeeding in today's age of artificial intelligence networking if they put their attention toward cultivating genuine ties with one another and making contributions to the accomplishments of others.

Chapter 9

The Gig Economy: Harnessing the Power of Freelance Work

Because it provides individuals with opportunities for flexibility, freedom, and autonomy in their work, the gig economy has become an increasingly popular option for individuals to make a living. This chapter will present an overview of the gig economy, including its advantages and disadvantages, as well as tactics for achieving success in the realm of freelance employment.

What exactly is the "gig economy," though?

The phrase "gig economy" refers to a labor market in which the majority of workers do not have regular employment but instead engage in work on a freelance or contract basis for brief periods of time. Workers who participate in the so-called "gig economy" are frequently referred to as "gig workers" or "freelancers." Providing creative or professional skills such as writing or graphic design are examples of types of gig employment. Other examples include driving for ride-sharing services, delivering groceries or meals, and delivering groceries.

The Benefits and Drawbacks of Working Freelance

Working in the gig economy comes with its fair share of benefits as well as challenges, just like any other type of employment arrangement.

Pros:

Flexibility: Freelancers are in charge of their own work schedules and can pick when they want to put in their hours.

Autonomy is the state of having control over one's own work and being one's own employer. This enables gig workers to work on projects that they find interesting or satisfying.

Freelancers have the ability to work on a wide variety of projects for a wide variety of clients, which keeps their work interesting and varied.

Work that is performed remotely There are a variety of gig tasks that can be completed remotely, enabling freelancers to work from whatever location they want.

Cons:

Uncertainty:

Freelancers do not have a guarantee of a consistent income or job stability, and their incomes may fluctuate based on the amount of work that is available.

Benefits: Gig workers are not eligible for standard employment benefits such as health insurance, paid time off, or retirement benefits. Benefits may include paid time off, vacation pay, and retirement benefits.

Isolation Freelancers often work alone and lack the social relationships that come with working in traditional office contexts. As a result, they may experience feelings of isolation.

Self-promotion: Gig workers are responsible for marketing themselves and finding new clients, which may be an arduous process that takes a lot of time and can be difficult.

Methods for Achieving Victory in the Freelance Workforce

Create a Niche:

Freelancers who want to stand out from the crowd and attract customers may consider developing a specialty in a particular area of expertise or skill.

Build a Professional Network Freelancers should make an effort to develop relationships with other professionals working in their field, as well as look for possibilities to work together with others and gain knowledge from them.

Establish a Powerful Online Presence Freelancers can increase their chances of landing clients by creating a professional website, maintaining an active presence on social media, and maintaining an online portfolio of their work.

Freelancers need to do their homework and find out what the going rate is for their services in the market before they can come up with prices that are reasonable for both themselves and their customers.

Invest in Your Professional Development Freelancers should always be working to enhance their skills and knowledge. They may do this by enrolling in classes or attending seminars in order to keep up with the latest trends and best practices in their sector.

Carefully Manage Your Finances Freelancers should maintain proper financial records, save money each month for their taxes, and seriously consider seeking the assistance of a financial counselor or accountant for assistance with managing their finances.

create Self-Care a Priority In order to avoid burnout and maintain mental and physical health, freelancers should create time in their schedules for activities that fall under the category of self-care, including as exercise, hobbies, and socializing.

Those who are interested in freelancing will find that the gig economy presents them with a variety of opportunities as well as problems. It is vital to develop a niche, build a strong professional network, create a powerful web presence, set rates that are reasonable, invest in professional growth, carefully manage finances, and emphasize self-care in order to flourish as a gig worker. If individuals do so, they will be able to harness the potential of the gig economy and establish careers that are both gratifying and sustainable for themselves.

Chapter 10

Entrepreneurship: Turning Ideas into Reality

The act of seeing a lucrative new business opportunity, launching it, and growing it into a successful enterprise is an example of entrepreneurial activity. People who recognize opportunities and are willing to take calculated risks in order to create value for themselves and others are called entrepreneurs. In the following chapter, we will discuss the qualities that define successful business owners, the obstacles that they encounter, and the actions that you can take to transform your own ideas into a profitable enterprise.

The Characteristics of Successful Business Owners

1. Many of the world's most successful businesspeople have similar qualities that have helped them thrive in today's cutthroat corporate environment. Among these characteristics are:

2. Entrepreneurs are visionaries because they have the capacity to spot opportunities and imagine a more favorable future, and they also have the tenacity and desire to turn that better future into a reality.

3. Entrepreneurs are known for their willingness to take risks and their lack of fear of failing since they view failure as a valuable learning experience.

4. Entrepreneurs are driven by a strong commitment to their company and a willingness to invest the time and energy required to see it through to a successful conclusion.

5. Entrepreneurs are flexible and able to adapt their business strategies as necessary to respond to changes in the market or business environment. Adaptability is a key characteristic of successful entrepreneurs.

6. Entrepreneurs have the ability to overcome setbacks and hurdles, as well as keep their passion and focus even when they are confronted with hardship.

The Obstacles That Entrepreneurs Must Overcome

Starting a business on one's own may be both challenging and risky.

Because starting a business requires a significant investment of time, money, and other resources, business owners are usually forced to make due with less resources than they would prefer.

Ambiguity: Because the future is never predictable, entrepreneurs must be able to handle ambiguity while yet taking reasonable risks.

Because of the tremendous level of rivalry that exists in the business world, entrepreneurs must be able to distinguish themselves from their contemporaries in order to be successful.

Regulation: In order to manage a business lawfully and ethically, business owners must adhere to a plethora of legal and regulatory norms, which can be challenging and time consuming.

The process of managing growth necessitates that business owners successfully manage their resources and ensure that they can scale up their operations to meet increasing client demand as their enterprises expand.

How to Take Your Concepts and Turn Them Into a Profitable Business

There are a number of important measures that need to be taken in order to transform your ideas into a profitable commercial enterprise if you are considering going into a company for yourself. These steps are as follows:

1. Carry Out Extensive Market Research Before launching your company, it is essential to carry out extensive market research in order to find potential clients, evaluate the competition, and determine whether or not your business idea will be successful.

2. Create a Business Strategy It is absolutely necessary for any new firm to have a comprehensive business strategy. Your business plan should provide an overview of your company's objectives, primary target market, significant competitors, marketing and sales tactics, financial predictions, and other important particulars.

3. Acquire Funding: Establishing a new company almost always necessitates the acquisition of financial resources. It's possible that you'll need to take out a loan for your company, look for financing from venture capitalists or angel investors, or use your personal funds to finance your business.

4. Construct Your Team: As your company expands, you will need to construct a team consisting of employees or independent contractors to assist you in the management of your operations. It's possible that this will need recruiting people with particular talents or handing off work to independent contractors.

5. Launching Your Company and Beginning to Market It Once you have developed your business plan and identified prospective sources of

finance, it is time to launch your company and begin marketing it to people who might become consumers. This may involve developing a website, marketing through social media platforms, advertising, or utilizing one of several other tactics.

Conclusion

Those who are prepared to put in a lot of effort and take risks in order to make their ideas a reality may find success in the difficult but rewarding field of entrepreneurship. Successful entrepreneurs have critical characteristics such as vision, willingness to take risks, passion, adaptability, and resilience. They must also be able to negotiate problems such as limited resources, unpredictability, competition, regulation, and the capacity to manage growth.

Chapter 11

Remote Work: Thriving in a Digital World

With the advent of AI and other cutting-edge technology, remote work has become increasingly popular in recent years. This chapter will help you flourish as a remote worker in the age of AI by providing advice on how to thrive in the virtual workplace. We'll also provide examples of people who have made the transition to working remotely successfully.

Preparing Your Office Environment

It is essential to your success as a remote worker that you establish a work environment that allows you to relax while yet being productive.

Set aside a specific room in your house as your office, preferably one that is isolated from your main living quarters.

Put money into ergonomic necessities like a supportive chair, an adjustable desk, and a screen at eye level.

Make sure you have access to a fast and dependable internet connection, as well as any other required devices or software.

In the real world:

Graphic designer Jane set up shop in her spare bedroom, complete with a big desk, comfortable chair, and high-resolution screen. She has been much more productive since setting up a private office where she is free from interruptions.

Time Management

You'll need to be able to manage your time well if you want to be successful in a remote work environment, where you also have personal obligations.

Establish a schedule that includes time for work, breaks, and relaxation.

Make good use of time management and organization resources such as calendars, to-do lists, and mobile time monitoring applications.

Establish attainable objectives and timeframes, and keep your colleagues and superiors updated on your progress.

In the real world:

Mark, a remote software developer, manages his time efficiently with the Pomodoro Technique. So that he doesn't lose focus or get burned out, he divides his daily into 25-minute work sessions separated by 5-minute breaks.

Maintaining Contact with Your Group

Working remotely with artificial intelligence-powered technologies and tools increases the importance of clear communication and close teamwork.

Email, instant messaging, and video conferencing are just some of the digital channels you can use to keep in touch with your coworkers.

Plan regular meetings and updates to keep the lines of communication open and the team spirit high.

Make sure your coworkers and superiors are aware of your contributions and development by actively seeking feedback and delivering updates on your work.

In the real world:

Lisa, a marketing expert who works remotely, schedules weekly virtual team meetings to keep everyone apprised of progress, generate new ideas, and foster team spirit. She keeps her team energized and committed by encouraging communication and collaboration.

Learning to Work Independently

You'll need to hone a set of talents and abilities unique to your career and the online workplace if you want to succeed while working from home.

Work on improving your communication abilities, as this is one of the most important aspects of working remotely.

Increase your proficiency in the digital realm by learning how to use a variety of remote-working software, apps, and platforms.

Gaining the ability to self-motivate and self-discipline is essential if you want to be productive while working from home.

In the real world:

Tom, a distant project manager, understood the significance of good writing and decided to take a course to hone his abilities in this area. His team is now better able to work together because his emails and project updates are clearer and more concise.

Maintaining a Healthy Work-Life Balance

As a remote worker, your health and happiness depend on your ability to strike a good work-life balance.

Limit your job hours so that you can spend time on things that are important to you, including family and hobbies.

Avoid exhaustion by taking frequent breaks throughout the day.

Take care of yourself:

To keep your mind and heart-healthy, pick back up where you left off with activities like physical activity, meditation, and socializing with loved ones.

Keeping a good work-life balance is important for everyone, and Emily, a remote customer service representative, does it by strictly limiting her work time. She works out first thing in the morning, takes a half hour for lunch and a half hour for a walk, and is done with her day by 6 o'clock. As a result, she has more time in the evenings to spend with her loved ones and pursue activities that bring her joy and refresh her spirit.

Adjusting to Artificial Intelligence While Working From Home

To be competitive in the modern workforce, remote employees must learn to use and adapt to artificial intelligence technologies.

Keep up with the latest research in AI and how it might affect your field.

Master the ins and outs of working with tools and systems powered by artificial intelligence.

Take advantage of AI to boost output, simplify procedures, and come up with novel ideas for your projects.

In the real world:

David, a remote data analyst, keeps up with AI developments by engaging in online discussions, watching webinars, and going to online conferences. By learning to use the most cutting-edge AI-driven tools, he has been able to automate mundane activities and free up time for more strategic and creative endeavors.

Success in the virtual office calls on a range of skills, including those related to organization, time management, communication, skill building, and juggling personal and professional obligations. Using the advice and tactics shown here, as well as the real-world examples provided, you will be able to thrive in a remote work setting and make the most of AI in your professional life.

Chapter 12

Navigating the Job Market: Modern Job Search Strategies

Finding the right job in today's world, which is increasingly driven by AI, can be a challenge, but it can also be rewarding. Traditional approaches of finding a job, such as looking through the classified ads in newspapers or depending on only one online job board, are no longer sufficient. Professionals are required to adopt and accept new job search tactics if they wish to successfully traverse the job market and secure the appropriate role for themselves. This chapter will discuss modern techniques to getting employment, and it will offer advice on how to make the most of these strategies while you are looking for a job.

Improve the quality of your online presence.

A robust web presence is absolutely necessary for anybody looking for work in the modern era. Because potential employers seek for candidates online, it is crucial to portray a professional and polished image across all platforms. This is especially important when applying for jobs.

You should add a professional photo, headline, and summary to your LinkedIn profile that shows your abilities, experience, and career objectives.

Sharing content that is relevant to your sector on social media platforms such as Twitter and Facebook will demonstrate both your expertise and your passion for the work that you do.

Keep up a personal website or an online portfolio that highlights your work, projects, and achievements.

Utilize Job Search Engines and Aggregators to Your Advantage

You can broaden your search and increase the likelihood of landing the ideal position by using job search engines and aggregators to locate listings for available positions from a variety of different sources.

Make use of job search engines such as Indeed, Glassdoor, and Simply Hired to locate job postings that may be found on a variety of websites and job boards.

You can receive updates about new job listings that meet your requirements by subscribing to relevant RSS feeds or setting up email alerts.

Make use of the advanced search facilities to narrow down your options for available jobs based on criteria such as area, industry, and job title.

Utilize the Job Market That Is Often Overlooked

Accessing the "hidden job market" is essential in order to discover more prospects because many job openings are never publicized to the general public.

Build contacts with other professionals working in the industry you want to break into by going to events, conferences, and meetups. This will allow you to find out about unadvertised employment positions.

Make touch with the people you already know and ask them for recommendations or introductions to companies that could be interested in hiring you.

It is a good idea to conduct informative interviews with people working in the area you are interested in breaking into so that you may get insights and create contacts that could lead to career chances.

Personalize the materials for your application:

Personalizing your resume and cover letter for each position you apply for will help you stand out in today's fiercely competitive job market by highlighting the abilities and experiences that are most pertinent to the role you are seeking.

Conduct an analysis of the job description, highlighting the terms and phrases that best define the needed qualities as well as the duties associated with the position.

Include these keywords in your resume and cover letter, stressing the talents and experience that are relevant to the position you are applying for.

Conduct research on the organization as well as its culture, and change the tone and content of your application materials so that they are in line with the organization's core values and expectations.

Get ready for the enhanced use of AI in recruitment:

As the use of recruitment tools driven by artificial intelligence (AI) becomes more widespread, it is necessary for job searchers to understand these technologies and to prepare for them.

Your resume should be optimized for applicant tracking systems (ATS) by using important keywords from the job description, using language that is clear and succinct, and organizing your resume in an organized manner.

Be ready for interviews that use artificial intelligence, such as video interviews powered by AI for facial analysis or screening interviews conducted by chatbots.

Maintain your awareness of recent advances in the use of AI in hiring, and modify your approach to finding work in accordance with the arrival of new technologies.

Continue to Follow Up and Be Persistent

Your enthusiasm in the role as well as your dedication to landing employment can be demonstrated by your persistence and follow-up during the job search process, which can make a difference.

Within the following twenty-four hours, you should send the people who interviewed you a thank-you email in which you reiterate your interest in the position and show your appreciation for the opportunity.

In the event that you have not received a response within the allotted amount of time, it is OK to send a follow-up email or make a courteous phone contact to inquire about the next steps in the recruiting process.

Maintain a dogged determination in your job hunt, applying for a variety of available jobs, and continually adjusting your strategy in response to the comments and data you collect.

To successfully navigate the new labor market, one must adopt an approach that is both strategic and flexible.

You can increase your chances of securing the ideal role in today's competitive job market by optimizing your online presence, utilizing job search engines and aggregators, tapping into the hidden job market, customizing your application materials, preparing for AI-enhanced recruitment, following up, and remaining persistent. All of these strategies involve the use of the Internet to find jobs. Adopting these contemporary techniques and maintaining a proactive stance in your job hunt can equip you to be successful in a world of work that is increasingly dominated by AI.

Chapter 13

Crafting an AI-Proof Resume: Standing Out from the Competition

Since the advent of artificial intelligence (AI), resumes have taken on an even greater significance in terms of their importance in differentiating candidates from one another. It is crucial to understand how these systems work and what you can do to improve your resume for AI systems because a growing number of firms are now using AI tools to filter resumes. In this chapter, we will discuss the numerous components that give a resume the ability to withstand being analyzed by AI, as well as provide you with some helpful pointers that will enable you to write an impressive resume that will be noticed.

Understanding the Role of AI in the Screening Process for Resumes

The process of hiring new employees has been revolutionized by artificial intelligence, making it possible for businesses to analyze resumes more quickly and accurately. However, it is essential to keep in mind that the data that is used to train AI can only determine how effective it ultimately is. If the AI system is trained on data that is either biased or incomplete, then it is possible that it will not be able to effectively identify the best candidates for a position.

When it comes to the process of reviewing resumes, AI will often search for particular keywords and phrases that are relevant to the job description. After that, the algorithm provides each resume with a score based on the degree to which it corresponds to the requirements of the job. The resumes that received the highest rankings are then given a more thorough assessment by a human recruiter.

Advice and Methods for Creating a CV that Can Compete with Computer Programs

To produce a resume that is unreadable by AI, you will need to concentrate on two primary aspects: the content of the document, as well as its formatting. The following are some suggestions that will assist you in maximizing both:

Use Relevant Keywords

AI performs a search for particular terms and phrases that correspond to the job description, as was described earlier. Make it a point to include relevant

keywords in your resume, but avoid using too many of them. Make sure to incorporate them in a way that is both natural and strategic throughout your resume.

Personalize your resume for each position that you apply to.

It's important to tailor your resume to each individual job that you apply for, even if it can be tempting to use the same CV for all of your applications. You should familiarize yourself with the job description and then modify your resume so that it highlights the aspects of your experience and expertise that are relevant to the position.

Put the spotlight on your accomplishments.

Instead of just describing your job responsibilities, focus on your successes and the things you've accomplished in your career. Employing numerical and statistical methods will help you quantify your achievements and illustrate your value to prospective employers.

Use Simple Formatting

When it comes to putting together your CV, keeping things as simple as possible is essential. Make sure to use a typeface that is uncomplicated and simple to read, and try to limit the number of visuals and images you include. Make sure that your CV is neat, well-organized, and contains lots of white space to make it simple for an AI to read.

Stay away from Graphics and Images That Aren't Necessary.

Although using visuals and photographs on your CV can make it more aesthetically attractive, doing so may also mislead AI systems. Stick to a clear and uncomplicated structure that consists solely of text, and preserve the creative components for your personal website or portfolio.

Avoid the Use of Tables and Columns.

You should avoid utilizing tables or columns in your resume because AI has trouble comprehending documents formatted in that manner. Use bullet points or a straightforward, chronological arrangement in its place to make it simpler for AI to read.

Make Sure to Double-Check Your Spelling and Grammar.

It is still important to verify your spelling and punctuation, even though AI is developed to search through resumes for certain terms and phrases. Errors can make your resume look amateurish and increase the likelihood that it will be ignored by AI systems.

Maintain a Current Version of Your Resume.

In conclusion, it is essential to keep your CV current at all times. Maintaining an up-to-date CV that highlights your most recent accomplishments, experiences, and talents is essential, as is tailoring it to each position for which you are applying.

In today's highly competitive job market, it is crucial to distinguish out from the competitors by developing a CV that is immune to being analyzed by AI. You can improve your chances of getting discovered by potential employers by learning how AI systems function and then tailoring your resume for AI use. Focus on incorporating important keywords, tailoring your resume for each job you apply for, highlighting your accomplishments, utilizing a basic structure, and staying away from superfluous visuals or images in your resume. You'll be able to craft an appealing CV with the help of this advice and methods, which can Highlight your transferable skills It is essential to highlight your transferable skills in order to make your resume stand out from the rest of the applicants' resumes. Transferable talents are skills that you may have developed in one situation, but which can also be employed in other circumstances. For example, if you have worked as a customer service representative, you have developed outstanding communication, problem-solving, and interpersonal skills. These talents are valuable in a variety of other sectors as well, including marketing, sales, and human resources, among others. Therefore, make sure that your resume highlights these skills that may be applied in a variety of settings.

In spite of the fact that AI may be very good at processing data, it is unable to comprehend human feelings and qualities like empathy, creativity, and leadership. Therefore, it is important to place an emphasis on these human attributes. Because of this, it is essential to highlight these human traits in your resume in order to differentiate yourself from the other applicants. Put an emphasis on the accomplishments that demonstrate your ability to empathize with clients, your inventiveness in finding solutions to problems, and your leadership abilities in managing teams.

Use keywords: a lot of organizations are now using artificial intelligence-based applicant tracking systems (ATS) to weed out resumes based on certain keywords. Therefore, it is extremely important to make use of pertinent keywords in your resume that are particular to the position for which you are seeking. Conduct research on both the job description and the website of the organization to locate keywords that are associated with the position. Be sure to incorporate these keywords throughout your resume, but notably in the section devoted to your qualifications and talents.

Personalize your resume:

One of the most effective ways to distinguish yourself from the other candidates is to personalize your resume to reflect the particular job for which you are applying. This requires you to tailor your CV to meet not only the job description, but also the culture of the organization and the field. Spend some time learning about the firm as well as the specifications of the position in order to get a better idea of what the potential employer is seeking. Make use of this information to personalize your CV and highlight the aspects of your talents and experiences that are most pertinent to the job.

To differentiate oneself from the other candidates in this day and age of artificial intelligence (AI), it is absolutely necessary to write a resume that is immune to the effects of AI. You may improve your chances of being discovered by potential employers by optimizing your resume with the appropriate keywords, stressing your transferable abilities and human qualities, and personalizing your resume to reflect the particular position for which you are applying. This will help employers find your resume more easily. AI may be powerful, but it lacks the human touch that gives us our distinctive identity. Because of this, it is essential to place an emphasis on the aspects of your personality that set you apart from the other candidates and provide you an advantage over them.

Chapter 14

Mastering the Interview: Selling Your Skills in a New Era

The process of being interviewed for a job can be nerve-wracking, especially in this day and age of artificial intelligence and automation. The interview process has changed as a result of improvements in technology; as a result, job applicants need to be ready to participate in a variety of new and unique forms of interviews. In this chapter, we will discuss how to effectively prepare for and dominate the interview process. We will also go over some helpful hints on how to sell your skills and differentiate yourself from the competition.

The Development of the Questioning and Interviewing Process

The interview procedure has changed throughout the years, and now, as a result of advances in technology, it is undergoing yet another transformation. The following is a list of some of the most recent developments in the interviewing process:

Video Interviews:

With the introduction of video conferencing, many businesses are employing video interviews as a way to screen candidates before inviting them for an in-person interview. This is done through the use of video conferencing.

Behavioral Interviews:

The primary goal of behavioral interviews is to learn how candidates have responded in the past to a variety of scenarios. These kinds of interviews are gaining popularity because they give potential employers a better insight of how candidates may perform in the future on the job.

Interviews Conducted with the Assistance of AI Presently, several businesses are beginning to use AI to assist in conducting interviews. The use of chatbots to conduct early screenings or the application of AI to assess a candidate's speech patterns and body language are two examples of this.

The Process of Getting Ready for the Interview

In this day and age of artificial intelligence and automation, it is more important than ever to prepare for an interview. Here are some suggestions to assist you in getting ready:

Conduct Research on the firm Before the Interview Conduct as much research as possible about the firm you will be interviewing with. This includes information about the company's mission and principles, as well as any current news or initiatives they've been working on.

Examine the Detailed Job Description:

Be sure that you have a solid understanding of the job requirements, as well as how your previous experience and talents compare to those needs.

Practice Your Responses:

You should be ready to respond to questions that are asked frequently in interviews, such as "Tell me about yourself" or "What are your strengths and weaknesses?" Prepare in advance by practicing your responses.

Prepare Questions:

Make sure you have a list of questions ready to ask the person conducting the interview. This demonstrates your interest in the firm as well as the position that they are hiring for.

Attire de calibre professional:

Prepare for the interview by dressing appropriately. It's possible that this will change based on the culture of the firm, but in general, it's best to err on the side of being excessively formal.

How to Conquer the Job Interview

Following the completion of your preparation for the interview, the next step is to become an expert in the subject. Here are some suggestions that will help you stand out from the crowd:

1. Maintain Your Self-Confidence It is essential to maintain your self-confidence while being interviewed. Achieve a level of self-assurance regarding your skills and the contributions you can make.

2. Put Your Skills Front and Center: Be careful to showcase the skills you possess and how they connect with the needs of the job. To demonstrate that you are capable, provide concrete examples drawn from your previous work experience.

3. Be True to Yourself: Maintain your natural demeanor throughout the interview. Don't make the mistake of pretending to be someone you're not.

4. Pay Close Attention to This: Pay close attention to the questions posed by the interviewer and provide well-considered responses. Ask for clarification on an issue if you have any doubts regarding its meaning.

Exhibit Your Enthusiasm:

Exhibit a positive attitude toward both the position and the firm. The interviewer might form a favorable opinion of you as a result of this.

After the interview, make it a point to send a thank-you email or handwritten note to the person who interviewed you. This demonstrates that you are still interested in the employment, and it also helps the interviewer keep you at the forefront of their mind.

The interview process might be frightening, but if you properly prepare and approach it with the right mindset, you will be able to succeed. You may stand out during the interview and boost your chances of getting the job by doing research about the organization, practicing your responses, and emphasizing the abilities that you have to offer. Keep in mind that you should always follow up after the interview and that you should always be confident, sincere, and enthusiastic. If you follow these guidelines, you will be well on your way to achieving success in this day and age of artificial intelligence and automation.

Chapter 15
Negotiating Your Worth: Strategies for Compensation and Benefits

The process of negotiating wages and benefits might be intimidating, but it is an essential skill to master nonetheless. In this chapter, we will discuss the essential components of successful compensation and benefit negotiations in the modern labor market. We will talk about the value of your abilities and expertise, as well as the need of being prepared and communicating well. In addition, we will provide you some tactics that you can use to bargain with self-assurance and arrive to a positive conclusion.

Comprehending the Value That Is Placed on My Skills and Experience:

It is critical that you have a solid grasp of the market value of your experience and talents before engaging in any sort of negotiation. Carry out some research to determine the compensation range that is typical for roles of a comparable nature within your industry and location. Make use of online tools such as Glassdoor, PayScale, or LinkedIn compensation to obtain a sense of the typical compensation range associated with your employment. With the use of this information, you will be able to estimate a reasonable range for your pay.

Get Clear on Your Goals:

Before beginning a negotiation, it is essential to have a clear idea of what it is you wish to achieve. Find out what the bare minimum wage and benefits package is that you are willing to take, as well as what you would regard to be ideal. When determining the terms of your negotiation, you should take into account both your short-term and long-term professional ambitions.

Getting Ready for the Negotiation:

The key to good negotiation is thorough preparation. Do some preliminary research on the firm as well as the position you will be interviewing for. Learn as much as you can about their history, values, and goals. Find out what perks, such as health insurance, retirement programs, and paid time off, they provide for their employees. Create a list of the advantages and privileges that are most significant to you and prioritize them.

Participate in role-playing exercises with a trusted friend or advisor to hone your bargaining skills. Prepare answers to the often-asked questions and common objections that you might hear throughout the discussion. During the course of the negotiation, you should perfect both your body language and your tone of voice so that you can convey an air of self-assurance and assertiveness.

While the Negotiation Was Going On:

Always try to maintain your composure and self-assurance while you are haggling over your advantages and remuneration. To get started, begin by emphasizing your experience, talents, and qualifications. Discuss how you will contribute to the success of the organization and share examples of your previous accomplishments in this discussion.

Make sure you have a clear understanding of the wage range and benefits you are looking for. Make use of the research that you conducted as support for your claims. Give an explanation of how your expertise and skills justify the amount of money you want to be paid.

Pay close attention to the employer's response, and be willing to make concessions if necessary. Keep an open mind on the possibility of receiving additional benefits or pay in the form of different structures, such as performance-based bonuses or stock options. Keep in mind that the objective of the negotiation is to reach a solution that is advantageous to both parties.

Immediately Following the Negotiation:

After the negotiation is over, set aside some time to reflect on the agreement that was reached. Have you been able to get the income and benefits that you had hoped for? If not, you should think about the circumstances that contributed to the result. Make use of this experience to better prepare yourself for future conversations.

If you are offered the employment, you should thoroughly examine the remuneration package before deciding whether or not to accept it. Make sure that the salary and perks are satisfactory to you and that they are detailed in the contract. Do not be hesitant to inquire further for clarification if you have any questions or concerns.

In today's competitive employment market, the ability to negotiate one's salary and benefits package is an absolute requirement for professionals. You will be able to negotiate with confidence and come to an agreement that works in your favor if you first determine the value of your talents and expertise, then choose what you want, and then prepare for the negotiation. Remind yourself to have a level head and exude confidence throughout the discussion, pay close attention to how the employer responds, and be ready to make concessions. You will be able to negotiate a wage and benefits package that is reflective of your value as an employee and adds to your long-term career goals if you use these tactics.

Chapter 16

Embracing Workplace AI: How to Work Alongside Machines

Accepting Artificial Intelligence in the Workplace: Strategies for Collaborating with Machines

The way we work is being revolutionized by artificial intelligence (AI), which is automating formerly manual processes and enhancing human decision-making capabilities. In order for workers to maintain their competitive edge in the labor market, they will need to adopt artificial intelligence (AI) technologies and become familiar with how to collaborate with robots. In this chapter, we will explore how to work effectively with artificial intelligence (AI), provide recommendations on how to develop the skills necessary to flourish in an AI-enhanced work environment and analyze the advantages and disadvantages of using AI in the workplace.

The Workplace Impacts of Artificial Intelligence, Both Positive and Negative

In the workplace, artificial intelligence has the potential to boost productivity, efficiency, and accuracy; yet, it also offers some obstacles. The following is a list of some of the advantages and difficulties posed by AI in the workplace:

Benefits:

Automation of normal tasks Artificial intelligence has the ability to automate processes that are repetitive and laborious, freeing up people's time to concentrate on more complicated and creative endeavors.

Augmented decision-making refers to the use of artificial intelligence to assist workers in making decisions that are better informed by giving data-driven insights and predictions.

Increased productivity: Artificial intelligence can assist workers in completing jobs more quickly and effectively, hence lowering the amount of time and effort required to finish a task.

Accuracy enhancement: AI has the potential to lessen the occurrence of errors while simultaneously enhancing accuracy in activities such as data entry and analysis.

Challenges

Displacement of jobs:

Artificial intelligence has the ability to perform specific professions, which could result in workers having to acquire new skills or find new employment.

AI algorithms have the potential to be prejudiced, and if they are not created and controlled appropriately, they may reinforce the biases that are already present in society.

Risks to data privacy and security Artificial intelligence (AI) systems may be susceptible to cyberattacks, and these issues are becoming an increasingly pressing problem.

Ethical issues: The use of artificial intelligence in the workplace creates ethical issues, such as the application of facial recognition technology and the potentially inappropriate use of personal information.

Working Efficiently with Artificial Intelligence

Workers need to embrace the technology and learn how to use it to their advantage in order to work effectively with artificial intelligence (AI). The following are some helpful hints for cooperating productively with AI:

Workers should educate themselves on the possibilities and limitations of AI in order to gain a better understanding of how the technology may be utilized to improve their work and how it should be implemented.

Collaborate with machines: Employees should be trained on how to work cooperatively with AI in order to improve their level of productivity and their capacity to make sound judgments.

Gain technical expertise Workers need to gain technical expertise such as data analysis and programming in order to operate effectively with artificial intelligence (AI).

Workers need to concentrate on developing their "soft skills" such as communication and problem-solving in order to operate effectively in teams with both their coworkers and their machines.

Adopt a growth mindset and commit to lifelong learning Employees should commit to lifelong learning and adopt a growth mindset in order to keep up with the newest breakthroughs in AI and maintain their competitive edge in the workforce.

Developing Competencies Necessary for Working in an AI-Enhanced Environment

Workers need to continuously learn new skills and expand their knowledge base throughout their careers if they want to be successful in an AI-enhanced work environment. Workers need to possess the following abilities in order to be successful in an AI-enhanced work environment:

Technical skills In order to operate effectively with artificial intelligence (AI), workers should develop technical skills such as data analysis, machine learning, and programming.

Workers need to cultivate "soft skills" like communication, teamwork, and problem-solving in order to operate effectively with both other people and robots.

Ability to Adapt: As the use of artificial intelligence (AI) continues to expand, workers should have the ability to adapt and be willing to learn new abilities.

Creativity is an important skill for workers to have so that they can solve difficult challenges by capitalizing on the distinct advantages that humans and technology each offer.

Emotional intelligence: Workers should work on developing their emotional intelligence in order to work cooperatively with machines and colleagues, as well as to negotiate the ethical and social consequences of artificial intelligence.

Artificial intelligence is causing a sea change in the way we do our jobs, and if people want to maintain their competitive edge in the labor market, they will need to adapt to this new technology and figure out how to collaborate effectively with robots. by having an awareness of both the advantages and disadvantages of AI.

Strategies for Working Alongside AI

You can improve your productivity when working alongside AI in the workplace by utilizing the following strategies:

Educate yourself on the technology:

Make it a priority to educate yourself on the artificial intelligence (AI) technologies that are currently in use in your business and how they function. This information can help you understand how technology affects your role and how you can more successfully operate alongside it.

Adjust your mode of communication because it's possible that AI systems won't respond to communication in the same manner that people do. When interacting with AI, it is critical to ensure that your communication is both clear and succinct so that the system can comprehend what you are trying to say.

Practice your ability to think critically: artificial intelligence systems may be able to assist in the automation of mundane jobs, but they may not always be able to handle complicated problems. Developing your ability to think critically can help you determine areas in which artificial intelligence can be of assistance and those in which human judgment is still required.

Collaborate with artificial intelligence Instead of viewing AI as a threat to your employment, seek for methods to collaborate with the technology in order to obtain more desirable results. The use of artificial intelligence (AI) can provide insights and data that can help you make decisions that are better informed and improve your performance.

Maintain a teachable mindset since artificial intelligence is always improving and new systems are being developed all the time. You can stay ahead of the curve and maintain your competitive edge in the workplace by retaining a growth mindset and being willing to learn new skills and adapt to new technologies.

The whole character of work is being transformed by AI, and this trend will only accelerate in the years to come. Although the idea of working in close proximity with robots could be intimidating at first, adopting AI can result in a wide range of positive outcomes for both individuals and businesses. You will be able to successfully traverse the shifting environment of work and prosper in the age of AI if you learn critical skills, understand the potential and limitations of AI, and adopt methods for working alongside the technology.

Chapter 17

Balancing Work and Life: Strategies for Well-being

Finding a healthy balance between one's personal life and one's professional life in today's culture of work, which is fast-paced and demanding, can be challenging. It is vital to take proactive efforts to manage your time, preserve your well-being, and create a satisfying life that encompasses both professional and personal hobbies. As the boundaries between these two realms grow increasingly blurred, it is essential to take proactive steps to manage your time. This chapter will discuss methods for achieving a healthy work-life balance, including techniques for time management, establishing healthy boundaries, and placing an emphasis on both one's physical and emotional well-being.

Managing Your Time

Effective time management is one of the most important factors in maintaining a healthy work-life balance. The following is a list of techniques that will assist you in better managing your time:

Establish Priorities: Determine what aspects of your professional and personal life require the most of your attention and then schedule your time accordingly. To keep yourself organized and on track, it can be helpful to make use of several tools, such as calendars, to-do lists, and productivity apps.

Put Boundaries in Place: Create distinct separations between your job time and your personal time. For instance, try not to check your work email or answer work calls when you should be spending time with your family, and vice versa.

Delegating tasks and outsourcing them: In order to make more time for the things that are most important to you, you should learn to delegate chores at work and outsource personal tasks such as cleaning and running errands.

Take care not to overcommit: Be honest with yourself about how much you can get done in a single day or in a given week. You can prevent overcommitting yourself and experiencing feelings of overload by saying "no" to certain activities or initiatives that are not a top priority.

Putting Your Health First As A Priority

Taking care of both your physical and mental well-being is an additional critical component of having a healthy work-life balance. The following are some things you can do to put your health first:

Regular exercise has been proven to improve mood, lower stress levels, and enhance energy levels. If you want these benefits, exercise regularly. Find a physical activity that you take pleasure in doing and make it a standard part of your daily routine.

Take care of yourself by:

Set aside some time each day for things like meditation, yoga, or a long soak in a hot bath that will help you unwind and recharge your batteries.

Get Adequate Rest:

Aim to get between seven and eight hours of sleep every night in order to assist your body and mind recharge and remain awake during the day.

Maintain your connections:

Developing and sustaining ties with family and friends can give a source of support and connection that can assist you in navigating the challenges of both your professional and personal lives.

Finding Fulfillment

Maintaining a healthy work-life balance requires not just effective time management and putting your health first, but also the ability to derive satisfaction from both one's professional and personal endeavors. The following are some approaches that can assist you in attaining fulfillment:

Make time for the things that provide you joy and fulfillment outside of work, such as hobbies, interests, and activities that you enjoy doing in your spare time.

Setting clear goals for both your personal and professional life is more crucial than ever in today's fast changing work scene. With the rise of artificial intelligence and robotics, navigating the unpredictability and changes in the employment market can be difficult. A clear sense of direction, on the other hand, can provide a sense of purpose and desire to adapt and thrive in the face of these challenges.

Making sure your goals connect with your values and aspirations is an important stage in goal setting. It is critical to assess what is genuinely important to you and to develop attainable goals that support your long-term vision. This may entail reflecting on your passions and interests, assessing your strengths and limitations, and defining the skills and competencies you need to improve to attain your objectives.

While making and attaining goals can be thrilling, it's also important to recognize and celebrate your accomplishments along the road. Recognizing even minor victories can enhance your confidence and determination to keep working toward your goals. You may retain a positive outlook and stay motivated even when faced with adversity if you take the time to acknowledge your accomplishments.

Developing a grateful attitude is another great skill for cultivating a good outlook. This entails reminding yourself of all the reasons you have to be thankful, such as your excellent relationships, good health, and meaningful employment. Even in the face of adversity, you may build a sense of contentment and fulfillment by focusing on the positive aspects of your life.

Maintaining a healthy work-life balance is critical for general well-being, and it necessitates continual focus and effort. Effective time management is essential for making sure you have enough time for both work and leisure activities. It is also critical to prioritize your physical and mental health, whether through regular exercise, healthy eating habits, or self-care techniques like meditation or mindfulness.

Finding fulfillment in both your personal and professional passions might help you live a more fulfilled life. Outside-of-work hobbies can bring a sense of fulfillment and balance, as well as possibilities for personal growth and development.

As artificial intelligence continues to revolutionize the labor market, it's critical to stay up to date on the likely trends and developments that may affect your career. One expected trend is an expansion in the use of automation and artificial intelligence (AI) in numerous industries, which may result in the replacement of specific work types. However, as a result of these technological improvements, new job possibilities and sectors are likely to arise.

In the face of these developments, it's critical to remain adaptable and flexible, always evaluating your skills and competencies and finding areas where you need to upskill or reskill. Seeking training or educational options can assist you in remaining relevant and competitive in the employment market.

To summarize, setting clear goals, celebrating accomplishments, cultivating a grateful attitude, and keeping a healthy work-life balance are all critical components of a fulfilling life and career. You may prosper in a future where artificial intelligence is progressively being integrated into many businesses by staying updated about changes and trends in the job market and remaining adaptable and agile in the face of uncertainty.

Increased Automation It is highly possible that we will observe an increase in the amount of automation that is used in a variety of different industries. This will be one of the most significant changes. It is possible that this will result in the loss of some employment, particularly those that involve doing tasks that are repetitive or routine. On the other hand, it may also result in the creation of new occupations that require higher levels of expertise in domains like as robots, the development of AI, and data analysis.

Work from Home:

The COVID-19 pandemic has hastened the shift toward working from home, and it's likely that this trend will continue in the years to come. Companies are becoming more aware of the advantages of having a distributed workforce, which include lower overhead expenses and increased employee flexibility. As a consequence of this, an increasing number of jobs are anticipated to become compatible with working remotely, which will create new options for individuals who have a preference for working from home or who are constrained by other location requirements.

Work as a Freelancer The gig economy has been steadily expanding over the past few years, and it is anticipated that this trend will continue. People will have access to more options to work on a project-by-project basis as businesses become more accustomed to the concept of hiring freelancers and independent contractors. Because of this, there is increased flexibility; nevertheless, there is also decreased stability and security. This may be both a benefit and a curse.

Chapter 18

The Future of Work: What to Expect in the Coming Years

It is only natural to question what the future holds for the labor market as artificial intelligence continues to make strides toward its goals of advancing and transforming the way we do our jobs. As you negotiate the shifting terrain, it will be helpful to keep the following probable trends and developments in mind.

Increased Automation One of the most likely changes that will have the most significant impact is the rise of automation in a variety of different industries. This may result in the loss of some employment, particularly those involving duties that are repetitive or routine in nature. On the other hand, it may also result in the creation of new occupations that require higher levels of expertise in domains such as data analysis, the development of artificial intelligence, and robots.

The COVID-19 epidemic has accelerated the trend toward remote work, and it is expected that this tendency will continue in the future years. Many businesses are beginning to see the advantages of having a distributed workforce, which include lower overhead expenses and increased employee flexibility. As a consequence of this, an increasing number of jobs are anticipated to become amenable to remote work, so creating new options for individuals who would rather work from home or who are constrained in other ways by their physical location.

Gig Work: Over the past few years, the gig economy has shown consistent growth, and it is anticipated that this pattern will continue. People will have access to an increased number of opportunities to work on a project-by-project basis as businesses become more at ease with the concept of hiring freelancers and independent contractors. This results in increased flexibility, but it also results in less stability and security, therefore it can be seen as both a blessing and a burden.

Upskilling and reskilling:

As a result of automation and other technological breakthroughs, the job market is undergoing significant change. As a result, it is becoming increasingly

vital for workers to remain current with the most recent skills and technologies. Because of this, acquiring new skills or improving old ones will be necessary for everyone who wants to continue to be competitive in the employment market. To our good fortune, there is a plethora of available options, such as online classes, boot camps, and training programs.

Technical abilities will always be necessary, but soft skills are becoming increasingly crucial in today's competitive workplaces. The abilities of communication, teamwork, flexibility, and emotional intelligence are all included in this category. These human skills are going to become even more essential as AI and automation begin to take over more mundane activities.

Acceptance and Participation: We can anticipate that in the next years, a greater number of businesses will place a priority on diversity and inclusion in the workplace as more people become aware of how important these concepts are. This results in increased employment prospects for members of underrepresented groups as well as a more welcoming and equal working environment for all employees.

Taking Into Account Ethical Factors:

There will be a greater need to take into account various ethical factors as artificial intelligence (AI) continues to improve and become more widespread. Who, for instance, is to blame if a mistake made by an AI system results in someone else getting hurt? How can we make sure that artificial intelligence is used for the greater good and not simply for financial gain? These are difficult problems that, in the years to come, will call for a great deal of thoughtful study and consideration.

In conclusion, there is a good chance that the future of work will be characterized by a variety of significant changes, some of which include a rise in the use of automation, remote work, and gig employment. To be successful in this new era, workers will need to continue to develop their hard and soft talents while also keeping diversity, inclusiveness, and ethical considerations in the forefront of their minds. In the AI-driven economy of the future, it is feasible to be successful with the right amount of planning and preparation.

Chapter 19

Advocacy and Policy: Shaping the AI Landscape

I t is necessary to ensure that artificial intelligence and automation are created and deployed in a responsible and ethical manner in light of the continued expansion of their respective applications. For this reason, campaigning and policy initiatives will need to be made on both a local and a global scale.

When it comes to directing the development and application of artificial intelligence, governments at all levels have an important role to play. They can accomplish this through the establishment of legislative frameworks, the provision of funds for research and development, and the promotion of education and training programs designed to provide workers with the competencies required to flourish in an economy driven by artificial intelligence.

Collaboration is essential when working at the international level. It is imperative that governments and organizations from all around the world collaborate in order to establish and uphold standards for the ethical application of AI. This covers factors pertaining to issues of bias, discrimination, and privacy.

In order to shape the landscape of artificial intelligence, it is vital to consider the following:

The development and application of artificial intelligence (AI) should be guided by ethical principles to ensure that these technologies are produced and used in a responsible and ethical manner. This can be accomplished by establishing ethical guidelines. Concerns of privacy, openness, and responsibility need to be factored into the development of these principles.

Increasing diversity and inclusiveness: When developing AI systems, it is important to get input from a wide variety of stakeholders, including people of varying racial and gender identities as well as socioeconomic backgrounds. This has the potential to aid in the prevention of the development of AI systems that continue to promote discrimination and bias.

Protecting individuals' confidentiality and safety: Given the enormous amounts of data on which AI systems rely, it is very necessary to take the necessary precautions to ensure that this data is both preserved and put to the best possible use. For the purpose of preventing unauthorized access to sensitive information, stringent privacy and security precautions ought to be put into place.

Concerning the influence that AI and automation will have on jobs and the workforce as they continue to develop, it seems unavoidable that they will have some kind of effect on the labor force. It is imperative that enterprises and governments collaborate on the development of plans to ensure that workers are prepared with the skills necessary to flourish in an economy driven by artificial intelligence (AI).

Working together on research and development is essential if we want to make sure that artificial intelligence is developed in a way that is both responsible and ethical. It is imperative that governments, corporations, and researchers from all around the world collaborate in order to make strides forward in our knowledge of artificial intelligence (AI) and to establish the tools and standards necessary to mold its evolution and application.

How we decide to build and apply AI in the future will, in the end, determine the nature of work in the future. We are able to ensure that these technologies are utilized in a way that is beneficial to society as a whole if we advocate for rules and practices that are responsible and ethical.

Chapter 20
The Silver Lining: Finding Purpose and Passion after Job Loss

When you lose your work to artificial intelligence (AI), it can be a traumatic event that leaves you feeling disoriented, nervous, and uncertain about the future. Nevertheless, despite the fact that it may appear to be challenging, this experience may also be an opportunity to learn about new passions, reevaluate your job objectives, and design a life that is rewarding and which is in accordance with your beliefs and interests. In this chapter, we will discuss the positive aspects of being laid off and offer advice and direction on how to discover your purpose and passion in a world that is becoming increasingly dominated by artificial intelligence and automation.

Spend Some Time Thinking About It

Taking some time to reflect on what has happened to you is the first thing you should do when trying to locate the positive aspect of a negative situation. Ask yourself what you liked, what you found challenging, and what you didn't like about your prior employment. The answers may help you decide what you want from your next job. Think about the things that drove you and the things that made you feel like you'd accomplished something. You will gain a better understanding of what you actually value and what you want out of your next employment if you engage in this process of self-reflection.

As soon as you have a crystal clear grasp of your skills, interests, and core beliefs, you can begin looking into new opportunities that are congruent with those things.

Think About Changing Your Routine at Work

The threat of being replaced by AI at work may be a chance to investigate alternative lines of work that you had not previously explored. Artificial intelligence is having a transformative effect on a wide range of industries and spawning new career prospects that call for a different set of skills than those required for traditional occupations. Investigate several domains that are now making use of AI to determine whether or not these domains correspond to your interests and values.

Think About Signing Up for a Class.

Consider enrolling in a class if you discover that you need to acquire new abilities in order to investigate alternative avenues of professional development. You may learn everything from fundamental computer programming to more advanced skills such as machine learning and data analysis by taking one of the many available online courses. These courses range from the most fundamental computer programming to the most advanced. You may be able to acquire the skills necessary to pursue a different line of work by enrolling in a class.

Start a Side Hustle

Beginning a side business can be an excellent way to investigate the things that interest you and learn new skills. Your search for a new work can offer you with additional financial stability if you pursue a side hustle in the meantime. Think about opening a blog, a shop on Etsy, or working as a freelancer. Make sure that whatever you decide, it is in line with the things that are most important to you and your passions.

Establish Contacts and Look for Help

Building relationships is an essential component of looking for the silver lining in every situation. Make sure your family, friends, and coworkers are aware that you are on the hunt for a new job or investigating different avenues of professional development by reaching out to them. Attending business events and conferences is a great way to meet individuals in the subject that you are interested in. Join online communities that are focused on topics that interest you, and get involved in the conversations there.

During this period, it is essential to search for support from others. The experience of being laid off from work can be a trying and solitary one. Make an appointment with a therapist, a coach, or a mentor in order to receive advice and assistance.

Adopt a Growth Mindset and an Attitude Favoring Resilience

It takes resiliency and a growth mentality to find the positive aspects of a negative situation, such as losing your job. Take full advantage of the chances and difficulties that come along with this experience. Keep in mind that mistakes and setbacks are an inevitable part of the process of gaining new knowledge. Keep in mind the experiences you've had and the talents you've picked up, and use them as building blocks for your success in the future.

Conclusion

When you lose your work to artificial intelligence (AI), it can be a traumatic event. However, it can also be an opportunity to find new passions and reevaluate your career goals. Take some time to think, investigate other avenues for your profession, cultivate new talents, network with others, and look for support. Embrace resiliency and a growth attitude, and keep in mind that it is possible to discover the positive in any situation if you have the correct mindset and the support you need.

Summary of Key Takeaways

The readers of "I Lost My Job to AI...Now What?" have gained an understanding of the effects that artificial intelligence (AI) will have on the labor market as well as the ways in which they can adjust to the changes that will occur as a result of AI. The following is a list of some of the most important topics discussed in the book:

Already, AI is having an impact on a wide range of businesses and professions, and this trend is expected to continue over the next few years. It is essential to keep abreast of these shifts in the environment and devise tactics for negotiating them as they occur.

Adaptability is going to be one of the most important abilities in a world driven by AI. This includes having a disposition that is receptive to the acquisition of new knowledge, being adaptable to shifting circumstances, and being brave enough to try new things.

Learning throughout one's entire life is equally essential in this new environment. To maintain one's relevance in the labor market and one's ability to compete with others for available positions, it is essential to continually expand one's skill set and keep oneself abreast of developing technology.

In today's competitive employment market, it might be helpful for individuals to develop a powerful personal brand and network in order to differentiate themselves from the competition. This includes developing an impressive resume and online presence, as well as networking with other professionals in the business and peers in the same field.

In the event that you experience a loss of employment or a setback in your career, it is essential to have a positive attitude and be proactive. This may entail receiving support from loved ones, engaging in self-care practices, and looking for new chances for personal development and progress.

In its entirety, "I Lost My Job to AI...Now What?" highlights the significance of adaptation, skill growth, and lifelong learning in a society that is increasingly driven by AI. Readers can position themselves for success and fulfillment in their professions by embracing these values and taking proactive actions to navigate the changing job market. In doing so, they will position themselves to succeed in their careers.

Encouragement for the Journey Ahead

It is normal to feel overwhelmed and uncertain about the future as you begin this trip into a world of work that is affected by artificial intelligence (AI). This is because you do not know what the future holds. It is essential to keep in mind, however, that with every change comes a new opportunity.

You can open a universe of opportunities for both your personal and professional development if you take use of the potential of artificial intelligence (AI) and adjust to the new realities of the labor market. Bear in mind that the talents that are in demand in the market now may not be the same skills that will be in demand in the market tomorrow. As a result, it is absolutely necessary to consistently learn new abilities and be current on the most recent developments in the field.

It is also essential to keep in mind that the voyage might not go as smoothly as planned at all times. Along the path, there is a possibility that you will face difficulties and failures, but you should regard these problems as opportunities to learn and develop. As you make your way through this unfamiliar terrain, you shouldn't be afraid to ask for help from those you know, such as your friends, family, and coworkers.

Always keep an optimistic attitude and keep your attention fixed on the next prospects. You can build a rewarding and successful job in this age of artificial intelligence (AI) if you have the appropriate mindset and are able to adapt to changing circumstances. The future of work is always shifting, but if you are willing to adapt, you can make it happen.

Next Steps: Creating Your AI-Adaptation Plan

It is time to put what you have learned about how to adapt to this new reality into action now that you have a better knowledge of the influence that artificial intelligence will have on the job market and the techniques that will help you adapt to it. This chapter will assist lead you through the process of creating a personalized strategy for how you will adapt to a future driven by AI. It is crucial to build a plan for how you will adapt to a future driven by AI.

To begin, go back and look at the spreadsheets from Chapter 20, then modify them to fit your unique requirements and objectives. Think about the skills you already have and how they could be applied to new fields. Also think about any additional skills you might need to gain in order to keep up with the competition in the job market.

Establish objectives that are particular, measurable, and attainable in accordance with your values and desires. Create a timetable for reaching these objectives, breaking them down into more manageable tasks as you go. Be sure to keep track of your advancement and acknowledge your accomplishments along the road.

Keep in mind that the future dominated by AI will bring up new prospects for your career and personal development. Accept the changes that are happening and have an open mind to new adventures and tests. Maintain an open mind and a commitment to learning throughout your life.

You will be able to successfully navigate the shifting job market and find success in a world that is driven by artificial intelligence if you take these steps and create an AI-adaptation plan for yourself.

ADDITIONAL RESOURCES

The study of artificial intelligence is always progressing to new levels, so there is always more information to absorb. The following is a list of supplementary resources that can assist you in remaining current and enhancing your grasp of the realm of artificial intelligence;

Books:

"Artificial Intelligence: A Modern Approach" by Stuart Russell and Peter Norvig

"Superintelligence: Paths, Dangers, Strategies" by Nick Bostrom

"Machine Learning Yearning" by Andrew Ng

"The Hundred-Page Machine Learning Book" by Andriy Burkov

"The Fourth Age: Smart Robots, Conscious Computers, and the Future of Humanity" by Byron Reese

Online Courses:

Machine Learning on Coursera by Andrew Ng

Deep Learning on Udacity

Introduction to Artificial Intelligence on edX

Websites:

AI News

AI Trends

MIT Technology Review

Articles:

"The Ethics of Artificial Intelligence" by Nick Bostrom

"The AI Revolution: The Road to Superintelligence" by Tim Urban

"What Is Machine Learning?" by John Roach

These resources are just a starting point, and there are many more out there. By continuing to learn and grow, you can stay ahead of the curve in the age of AI.

In an Excel spreadsheet, the following is a list of the 50 jobs that are less likely to be replaced by artificial intelligence and the 50 jobs that perhaps could be replaced by AI:

Jobs Less Likely to be Replaced by AI	Jobs Possibly Replaced by AI
Actor	Accountant
Air Traffic Controller	Advertising Sales Agent
Animal Caretaker	Agricultural Worker
Artist	Assembly Line Worker
Athletic Trainer	Bank Teller
Childcare Worker	Bookkeeper
Chiropractor	Cashier
Clergy	Customer Service Representative
Coach	Data Entry Clerk
Counselor	Delivery Driver
Dental Hygienist	Dispatcher
Designer	Electrical/Electronic Technician
Editor	Financial Analyst
Engineer	Financial Clerk
Entrepreneur	Food Preparation Worker
Event Planner	Insurance Underwriter
Firefighter	Insurance Claims Clerk
Fitness Instructor	Loan Officer
Graphic Designer	Machinist
Hairdresser/Barber	Marketing Research Analyst
Human Resources Manager	Medical Assistant
Interior Designer	Medical Records Clerk
Interpreter/Translator	Meter Reader
Journalist	Paralegal/Legal Assistant
Librarian	Pharmacy Technician
Makeup Artist	Production Worker
Management Analyst	Real Estate Broker
Musician	Receptionist
Occupational Therapist	Retail Salesperson
Personal Trainer	Sales Representative
Physical Therapist	Secretary/Administrative Assistant

Physician	Shipping/Receiving Clerk
Plumber	Stock Clerk
Police Officer	Telemarketer
Project Manager	Travel Agent
Psychologist	Truck Driver
Public Relations Specialist	Typist/Word Processor
Registered Nurse	Warehouse Worker
Sales Manager	
Scientist	
Social Worker	
Software Developer	
Teacher	
Writer	

It is important to note that the following list is not inclusive and may be subject to change when new technologies related to AI become available. The concept of artificial intelligence taking over particular jobs does not necessarily indicate that those jobs would be completely eliminated; rather, the nature of the work may shift, which may call for a different set of skill sets. This is because artificial intelligence is still in its infancy. In addition, the likelihood of certain jobs being taken over by AI may vary from one sector of the economy to another, as well as depending on factors such as geography and other particulars of the profession in question.

Glossary

Artificial Intelligence (AI): The development of computer systems that can perform tasks that usually require human intelligence.

Machine Learning (ML): A subset of AI that uses algorithms to learn and improve from experience.

Deep Learning: A subset of ML that uses artificial neural networks to model and solve complex problems.

Natural Language Processing (NLP): A branch of AI that deals with the interaction between computers and human languages.

Robotics: The branch of technology that deals with the design, construction, and operation of robots.

Automation: The use of machines, robots, or technology to perform tasks without human intervention.

Industry 4.0: The fourth industrial revolution, characterized by the integration of digital technologies and advanced automation.

Digital transformation: The integration of digital technologies into all aspects of a business or organization.

Job displacement: The loss of jobs due to technological advancements, economic changes, or other factors.

Skill shift: The change in the demand for specific skills in the workforce.

Reskilling: Acquiring new skills or training to adapt to changes in the job market.

Up-skilling: Enhancing existing skills or developing new ones to remain competitive in the workforce.

Gig economy: A labor market characterized by short-term contracts or freelance work as opposed to permanent jobs.

Employment trends: Patterns or shifts in job growth, job loss, and overall changes in the workforce.

Job market trends: Patterns or shifts in the demand for specific jobs, industries, or skills.

Technical skills: Skills related to the use of technology, tools, or specific processes within a field or industry.

Coding languages: The languages used to write computer programs and software, such as Python, Java, or C++.

Data analytics: The process of examining, cleaning, transforming, and modeling data to extract useful information and insights.

Cybersecurity: The practice of protecting computer systems, networks, and data from theft, damage, or unauthorized access.

Cloud computing: The delivery of computing services, such as storage, processing, and software, over the internet.

Project management: The practice of planning, executing, and controlling projects to achieve specific goals and objectives.

Soft skills: Personal attributes or abilities, such as communication, teamwork, and problem-solving, that help individuals work effectively with others.

Hard skills: Technical or job-specific skills that can be taught or measured, such as programming or accounting.

Transferable skills: Skills that can be applied to multiple job roles or industries, such as project management or critical thinking.

Emotional intelligence: The ability to recognize, understand, and manage one's own emotions and the emotions of others.

Career adaptability: The ability to change and adjust to new job roles, industries, or career paths.

Lifelong learning: The ongoing, voluntary pursuit of knowledge and skills for personal or professional development.

Job satisfaction: The level of contentment or happiness one experiences in their job or career.

Creative professions: Jobs that involve the creation or expression of new ideas, such as writers, artists, or designers.

Empathy-driven careers: Jobs that require a high degree of empathy and compassion, such as counselors, therapists, or social workers.

Healthcare: The field of medicine and healthcare services, including doctors, nurses, therapists, and other healthcare professionals.

Education: The process of teaching, learning, and acquiring knowledge, skills, and values, often involving professionals such as teachers, trainers, and tutors.

Social work: A profession concerned with helping individuals, families, and communities improve their well-being and social functioning.

Human-centered design: An approach to designing products, services, or experiences that focuses on the needs and preferences of the people who will use them.

Entrepreneurship: The process of starting, organizing, and managing a business or venture.

Personal branding: The practice of marketing oneself and one's career as a unique brand, often through online presence and reputation management.

Online presence: The visibility and reputation of an individual or organization on the internet, often including social media profiles, websites, and blogs.

Social media: Online platforms that allow users to create and share content and engage in social networking, such as Facebook, Twitter, and LinkedIn.

Networking: The process of establishing and maintaining relationships with others in a professional context, often to exchange information, resources, and opportunities.

Elevator pitch: A concise, persuasive speech that communicates who you are, what you do, and what makes you unique, typically lasting about 30 seconds.

Thought leadership: The process of establishing oneself as an authority and expert in a particular field by sharing valuable insights and content with others.

Consistent messaging: Maintaining a clear and coherent message across all communication channels, both online and offline, to reinforce one's personal brand.

Networking strategies: Techniques and approaches for building and maintaining professional relationships, both online and offline.

Professional associations: Organizations that represent the interests of professionals within a specific industry or field and provide networking opportunities, resources, and support.

Online communities: Virtual spaces where individuals with shared interests or goals can connect, collaborate, and communicate, such as forums, discussion boards, or social media groups.

Mentorship: A relationship between an experienced professional (mentor) and a less experienced person (mentee) in which the mentor provides guidance, advice, and support.

Social capital: The value and benefits derived from one's social connections and relationships.

Relationship building: The process of developing and maintaining positive, mutually beneficial relationships with others.

Networking events: Professional gatherings designed to facilitate relationship-building and information exchange within a specific industry or field.

Continuous learning: The lifelong pursuit of knowledge and skills for personal or professional growth.

Professional development: Activities that enhance an individual's expertise within their profession.

Online courses: Internet-based educational programs offering self-paced learning.

MOOCs: Low-cost or free online courses open to anyone, often provided by universities.

Microcredentials: Short, focused courses resulting in certification or digital badges.

Learning communities: Collaborative groups sharing common interests or goals in learning.

Self-directed learning: The act of managing one's own learning experiences and goals.

Growth mindset: The belief that abilities can be developed and improved through effort.

Fixed mindset: The belief that abilities are innate and unchangeable.

Grit: The ability to persevere and commit to long-term goals despite challenges.

Perseverance: Persisting in the face of obstacles.

Adaptability: Adjusting and responding to changes and challenges.

Resilience: Recovering and bouncing back from setbacks.

Self-efficacy: Believing in one's ability to succeed and accomplish tasks.

Innovation: Introducing new ideas or methods that improve existing solutions.

Disruptive technologies: Technologies that significantly change industries or businesses.

Creativity: Generating new ideas or solutions to problems.

Design thinking: Empathetic, experimental problem-solving for user-centered solutions.

Problem-solving: Identifying and resolving challenges or issues.

Intrapreneurship: Applying entrepreneurial skills within an existing organization.

Intellectual curiosity: A desire to learn and explore new ideas or concepts.

Career planning: Setting and working towards professional goals throughout one's career.

Goal setting: Identifying specific, measurable, achievable, relevant, and time-bound objectives.

Work-life balance: Equilibrium between personal and professional responsibilities.

Career milestones: Significant events or achievements within one's career.

Personal fulfillment: Satisfaction and happiness from achieving goals or pursuing passions.

Career pivots: Changes in one's career path, often involving a shift in roles or industries.

Success metrics: Criteria used to measure progress and achievement in one's career.

Job search strategies: Techniques for identifying and pursuing job opportunities.

Applicant Tracking Systems (ATS): Software for managing and filtering job applications.

Resume optimization: Tailoring one's resume to specific job requirements for ATS scanning.

LinkedIn: A professional networking and career-related social media platform.

Job boards: Online platforms listing job openings and allowing users to search and apply.

Networking: Building and maintaining professional relationships.

Personal branding: Marketing oneself and one's career as a unique brand, often through online presence.

AI in HR: Using artificial intelligence to streamline human resources functions.

Recruitment technology: Tools and software for identifying, evaluating, and hiring candidates.

Candidate screening: Reviewing and assessing job applicants based on qualifications.

Video interviews: Remote interviews conducted via video conferencing software.

Chatbots: AI-powered software for engaging in conversations with users.

Predictive analytics: Using data and algorithms to make predictions about future outcomes.

AI ethics: Ensuring responsible, fair, and transparent AI development and use.

Bias in AI: Prejudice or discrimination within AI systems, often due to biased data.

Transparency: Openness and clarity in AI systems and decision-making processes.

Accountability: Responsibility for ethical AI development, deployment, and impact.

Data privacy: Protection of personal information collected, stored, and used by AI systems.

Regulation: Development and enforcement of laws governing AI technologies.

Fairness: Equitable treatment of individuals by AI systems, including efforts to mitigate bias.

Financial planning: Setting financial goals and developing a strategy to achieve them.

Budgeting: Creating and maintaining a plan for income, expenses, and financial goals.

Savings: Money set aside for future use, often in interest-bearing accounts.

Investments: Allocating

Source

rey, C. B., & Osborne, M. A. (2017). The future of employment: How susceptible are jobs to computerisation? Technological Forecasting and Social Change, 114, 254-280.

Bessen, J. E. (2019). AI and Jobs: The Role of Demand. NBER Working Paper No. 24235.

Arntz, M., Gregory, T., & Zierahn, U. (2016). The Risk of Automation for Jobs in OECD Countries: A Comparative Analysis. OECD Social, Employment and Migration Working Papers, No. 189.

World Economic Forum. (2020). The Future of Jobs Report 2020. Retrieved from https://www.weforum.org/reports/the-future-of-jobs-report-2020

Muro, M., Maxim, R., & Whiton, J. (2019). What jobs are affected by AI? Better-paid, better-educated workers face the most exposure. Brookings Institution. Retrieved from https://www.brookings.edu/research/what-jobs-are-affected-by-ai-better-paid-better-educated-workers-face-the-most-exposure/

Dweck, C. S. (2006). Mindset: The New Psychology of Success. Random House.

Bolles, R. N. (2021). What Color Is Your Parachute? 2022: Your Guide to a Lifetime of Meaningful Work and Career Success. Ten Speed Press.

Chamorro-Premuzic, T. (2013). Confidence: Overcoming Low Self-Esteem, Insecurity, and Self-Doubt. Hudson Street Press.

Dweck, C. S. (2006). Mindset: The New Psychology of Success. Random House.

Robbins, T. (2001). Awaken the Giant Within: How to Take Immediate Control of Your Mental, Emotional, Physical and Financial Destiny! Free Press.

U.S. Bureau of Labor Statistics. (n.d.). Occupational Outlook Handbook. Retrieved from https://www.bls.gov/ooh/

World Economic Forum. (2020). The Future of Jobs Report 2020. Retrieved from https://www.weforum.org/reports/the-future-of-jobs-report-2020

World Economic Forum. (2020). The Future of Jobs Report 2020. Retrieved from https://www.weforum.org/reports/the-future-of-jobs-report-2020

Institute for the Future. (2011). Future Work Skills 2020. Retrieved from http://www.iftf.org/futureworkskills/

McAfee, A., & Brynjolfsson, E. (2017). Machine, Platform, Crowd: Harnessing

Our Digital Future. W. W. Norton & Company.

Friedman, T. L. (2016). Thank You for Being Late: An Optimist's Guide to Thriving in the Age of Accelerations. Farrar, Straus and Giroux.

Wagner, T., & Dintersmith, T. (2015). Most Likely to Succeed: Preparing Our Kids for the Innovation Era. Scribner.

Pink, D. H. (2005). A Whole New Mind: Why Right-Brainers Will Rule the Future. Riverhead Books.

Ryan, R. L. (2016). How to Use Social Media in Your Job Search. CreateSpace Independent Publishing Platform.

Schawbel, D. (2011). Me 2.0: 4 Steps to Building Your Future. Kaplan Publishing.

Coursera. (n.d.). Retrieved from https://www.coursera.org/

edX. (n.d.). Retrieved from https://www.edx.org/

LinkedIn Learning. (n.d.). Retrieved from https://www.linkedin.com/learning/

Udemy. (n.d.). Retrieved from https://www.udemy.com/

Glassdoor. (n.d.). Retrieved from https://www.glassdoor.com/index.htm

Indeed. (n.d.). Retrieved from https://www.indeed.com/

Frey, C. B., & Osborne, M. A. (2017). The future of employment: How susceptible are jobs to computerisation? Technological Forecasting and Social Change, 114, 254-280.

Bessen, J. E. (2019). AI and Jobs: The Role of Demand. NBER Working Paper No. 24235.

Arntz, M., Gregory, T., & Zierahn, U. (2016). The Risk of Automation for Jobs in OECD Countries: A Comparative Analysis. OECD Social, Employment and Migration Working Papers, No. 189.

World Economic Forum. (2020). The Future of Jobs Report 2020. Retrieved from https://www.weforum.org/reports/the-future-of-jobs-report-2020

Muro, M., Maxim, R., & Whiton, J. (2019). What jobs are affected by AI? Better-paid, better-educated workers face the most exposure. Brookings Institution. Retrieved from https://www.brookings.edu/research/what-jobs-are-affected-by-ai-better-paid-better-educated-workers-face-the-most-exposure/

Dweck, C. S. (2006). Mindset: The New Psychology of Success. Random House.

www.ingramcontent.com/pod-product-compliance
Lightning Source LLC
Chambersburg PA
CBHW052338210326
41597CB00031B/5296